TOO CUTE

Amigurumi

30 Crochet Patterns for
Adorable Animals, Playful Plants,
Sweet Treats and More

Jennifer Santos

CREATOR OF SUPER CUTE DESIGN

PAGE STREET
PUBLISHING CO.

PAGE STREET
PUBLISHING CO.

First published in 2021 by

Page Street Publishing Co.

27 Congress Street, Suite 1511

Salem, MA 01970

www.pagestreetpublishing.com

Distributed by Macmillan, sales in Canada by The Canadian Manda Group.

25   24   23   22   21   1   2   3   4   5

ISBN-13: 978-1-64567-500-6

ISBN-10: 1-64567-500-9

Library of Congress Control Number: 2021937990

Cover and book design by Laura Benton for Page Street Publishing Co.

Photography by Jennifer Santos

Printed and bound in the United States

DEDICATION

To my always supportive husband: Thank you for understanding that yarn often needs to come before housework and for sharing your office with all my yarn.

Contents

INTRODUCTION

Welcome to a book full of cute and yummy amigurumi creations! I believe that everything is possible with a hook and some yarn, and that you can make any creation look super cute if you add a happy face to it. With this collection of adorable amigurumi dolls at your fingertips, I hope you'll soon feel the exact same way.

I started my amigurumi journey twelve years ago. The style of my work is inspired by the Japanese notion of kawaii or "super cute"—and that aesthetic is what I'm all about! I love adding cute faces to all my creations, which you will see throughout this book. I also have a huge sweet tooth, which is why so many of my designs are focused on yummy food.

I love to play with colors and to use unconventional color palettes. When people ask me what my favorite color is, I always say, "Rainbow!" I know it's not really a color, but I just can't pick one, and it's a huge reason why I love to design bright and colorful amigurumis! I can't wait for you to jump into the 30 cheerful designs that await you in these pages.

I want this book to be one you could pick up during your Netflix marathons, a book where the patterns are clear and not too complicated. A book that has quick projects as well as some that might be a little bit more challenging. While writing this book, I made sure it included a little bit of everything, which is why you will find savory foods, sweet treats, ice creams, cacti, animals and more. This book has everything—all with a smiling face!

Whether you are an experienced crocheter or new to amigurumi, there are plenty of projects in this book for you! Most of the patterns are beginner-friendly and work up quite quickly. Maybe you are looking to take a break from that blanket or sweater you have been working on for the last few weeks—why not pick up a cute project that you can finish in one evening? If you are a beginner, you will soon notice that most of the patterns only use single crochet and that the shapes are made either by increasing or decreasing the single crochet stitches. Once you get the hang of it, I'm sure you will be just as hooked on amigurumi as I am!

Before you dive into the patterns, you will also find some useful information for picking out your yarn, how to get the stuffing just the way you want it, embroidering the mouth, a great tip regarding safety eyes (Spoiler alert: It involves fire!) and more useful advice.

It is my hope that the patterns in this book will be pick-me-up projects to brighten your day, an extra dose of cuteness when you're feeling down or just a cute project for you to make to give to your loved ones.

Everything is possible with yarn, just let your imagination run wild!

And remember, everything is better with sprinkles!

Jennifer Santos

YARN SUGGESTIONS FOR PROJECTS YOU'LL LOVE

The best thing about amigurumi is that you can use basically any type of yarn you'd like!

All the projects in this book use Scheepjes Catona yarn in various colors. Scheepjes Catona yarn can be purchased online from yarn.com as well as lovecrafts.com. That being said, if you are having trouble sourcing Scheepjes Catona yarn, feel free to substitute it with any light fingering weight, cotton yarn of your choice.

It doesn't really matter what type of yarn you use; I personally prefer mercerized cotton yarn because it gives the stitches more definition. Acrylic yarn is also a good choice, as it's budget-friendly and can be found in many stores. Different types of wool yarn will also work well and will give your creations a fluffier, woolier look.

The exact yardage of yarn is not listed for the projects in this book because these items use up little yardage and can be made with less than one skein or hank of each color. This also makes amigurumi the perfect craft for using up leftover yarn, since you often do not need that much yarn for each project.

Gauge is also not critical when making amigurumi, just use a hook that matches you and your yarn. I've provided a suggested hook size for each project, but don't worry too much about it if you feel a different hook size will give you a better result. When I was first starting to make amigurumi, I noticed that my stitches were not tight enough, so if you are having that problem use a smaller hook size! The projects in this book are made using a US B/1 (2.25-mm) hook, which works well with light fingering weight yarn. Please note that if you are using a heavier weight yarn, you will need to increase the size of your hook as well. Remember also that the finished size of your creation will be different than the one listed in the patterns if you use a different hook size.

I also suggest colors for each pattern in this book, but don't feel like you have to follow my suggestions exactly. One of the most fun things about amigurumi is that you can let your imagination run wild!

TIPS FOR TACKLING EVERY AMIGURUMI CHALLENGE

My number one tip for adorable amigurumi is to have fun with it! Do not beat yourself up if your project does not come out the way you had initially expected, especially if you are new to making amigurumi. You should have seen my first dolls when I was just starting out—they were *not* cute. But if you just keep crocheting, you will get the hang of it—I promise!

ASSEMBLING

I'll be honest, the thing I like the least about making amigurumi is actually sewing everything together. That being said, my best tip for you is to take your time when assembling your amigurumi. Match your stitches as best as you can so that you sew into the matching stitches on each piece.

You will notice that it often states to leave a yarn tail at the end of each pattern piece, and you can then use those tails to sew the pieces together at the very end of each project.

Sometimes when I want a project to look really neat, I'll use sewing thread for assembling the pieces instead of the yarn tails. If you are planning to give a finished doll to small children, make sure to sew the pieces on very tight—you can also go over the stitches one extra time at the end for added security.

CHANGING COLORS

When changing colors, always be sure to do it on the last stitch before your color change. Work the last stitch until you have 2 loops left on your hook, then instead of the yarn you are currently working with, take your new yarn color and pull it through. This works for all stitches when changing colors—single stitch (sc), half double crochet (hdc) and double crochet (dc). Just pull your new color through the last 2 loops of the previous stitch, and your color changes will come out perfectly!

EMBROIDERING

When embroidering eyes or mouths, I use embroidery floss and a thin, sharp needle to get the precision I want. You will notice throughout the patterns that I suggest you should embroider the expressions onto the pieces before you have stuffed your creation. I prefer to do it this way so I can fasten the thread securely, and this way it will not come off. However, if you feel more comfortable with embroidering the mouth after you have stuffed your piece, you can also do it that way, too! As you get farther into your amigurumi journey, you'll learn your own preferences and be able to tailor the experience to suit you best.

INVISIBLE DECREASE

When making a decrease stitch, it can often create a visible bump in your piece, which is why I prefer to make invisible decreases instead of regular ones. An invisible decrease blends in better with the other stitches and will look much smoother.

To make an invisible single decrease stitch, insert your hook into the front loop of the next stitch (2 loops on your hook), then insert the hook in the next front loop (3 loops on your hook), then yarn over and pull through the first 2 loops (2 loops on your hook), yarn over and pull through the last 2 loops (like a regular sc)—and you have made an invisible decrease!

LOCKING STITCH MARKER

To keep track of where your rounds start and end, it is always helpful to use something like a stitch marker. You can use a regular locking stitch marker or a safety pin. You can also use a piece of contrasting yarn or even a bobby pin if those are all you have on hand! Just make sure to use something, or you will end up going crazy trying to figure out where the new round starts.

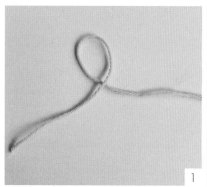
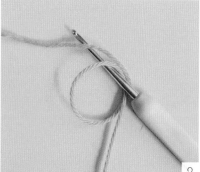
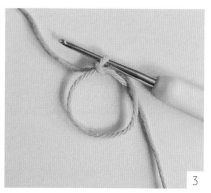
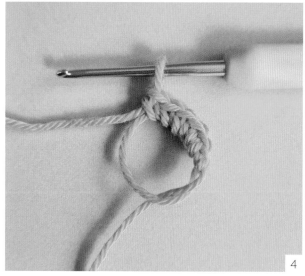
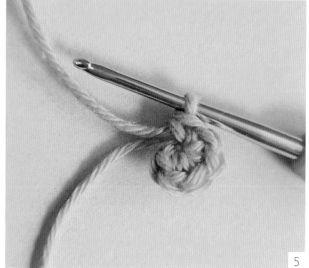

MAGIC RING

You will notice that almost all the patterns in this book start with a magic ring, also called a magic circle. It is an adjustable ring that works great when crocheting in the round. You work the first round of stitches into the ring, then pull one of the ends to tighten it. This will close the ring and there will be no space in the center of your project—sounds like magic right?

1. Cross the working end of the yarn over the tail to form a circle.

2. Now insert your hook into the ring and pull up a loop.

3. Chain 1 (this does not count as a stitch).

4. Crochet the stitches listed in the pattern. (For example, "6 sc into the magic ring.") You will crochet over both strands of the ring.

5. Tighten the ring by pulling the yarn tail.

SAFETY EYES

All the creations in this book have black safety eyes in sizes ranging from 4 to 8 mm. Safety eyes are great for amigurumi because you do not need to embroider the eyes on, but the eyes will still also stay put. Do note that even though they are safety eyes and should be very hard to pull off, you may not want to give creations with these to small children, since the small plastic eyes are a choking hazard. If you are planning to give your project to a young child and are looking for alternatives to using safety eyes, you can always embroider the eyes on, needle-felt the eyes on or sew on pieces of felt that have been cut into black circles.

My best tip when using safety eyes actually involves fire! I know, mixing yarn and fire—crazy, right? But it really does help! Once the backside of the safety eye has been attached, you can use a lighter to melt the excess piece on the back. You do need to be careful; you only need to hold the flame over it for a short time to make the plastic soft enough to flatten. Press it flat with the backside of your lighter or anything hard. This will make the surface flat on the back, which will prevent the stuffing from getting stuck between the eyes (this would make the eyes press outward).

STUFFING

When I first started making amigurumi, I often found that stuffing my pieces was the most difficult part. I had a hard time getting the stuffing into the smaller spaces, and it would come out either overstuffed or stuffed too loosely.

With this in mind, a chopstick is your best friend when stuffing amigurumi—it lets you stuff even the smallest pieces! When using a chopstick, you can reach all the way in and get the stuffing exactly where you want it to be.

While stuffing your projects, you want to stuff firmly so the amigurumi keeps its shape, but do not overstuff, otherwise it will stretch the fabric and the stuffing will show through. Use small amounts of stuffing at a time, and go slowly until you have the perfect level of squishiness. If you think that your stuffing is getting lumpy, you can roll the stuffed amigurumi against your hands to make it smoother.

In this book, I also use cardboard in the bottom of the designs that need to stand flat.

You can also put rice in the bottom of your pieces to give them more weight to stand up properly.

Anything Is Popsicle!

FROZEN TREATS TO MELT YOUR HEART

This chapter is all about the sprinkles as you stitch your way through five adorable ice cream-inspired projects! That's something to celebrate, right? While I know crochet ice cream is not the same as real ice cream, it sure is a pretty close second, don't you think? In this chapter, you will find patterns to make three different types of popsicles, a sundae and an ice cream cone. And to make these projects extra cute, they are animal hybrids as well! Adding a dose of creature-cuteness is one of my favorite things to do with amigurumi, and I know you'll love these projects as much as I do!

One pattern that I adore—and I hope you will, too—is the Double the Fun Popsicle (page 18). The color combinations for this pattern are almost endless! And you know what? You can skip the part where you sew them together, and you'll have a whole new design with a single popsicle! The Magical Unicorn Popsicle (page 15) and the Bubbly Bunny Popsicle (page 21) use almost the same pattern, but by adding different ears and accessories they become two different designs. I'm sure you can come up with lots more animal popsicles, too! What about adding the panda ears and eyes from the Three-Scoop Ice Cream Cone (page 25) to make an adorable panda popsicle?

Magical Unicorn Popsicle

This Magical Unicorn Popsicle is a pretty easy and quick project! It's made in one main piece, then the raspberry sauce and other decorations are made separately and sewn on. Think of this popsicle as magic on a stick! Use your imagination and make it in your own favorite colors, and why not add some glitter yarn? Because everything is better when it sparkles!

SKILL LEVEL: BEGINNER

MATERIALS

Light fingering weight yarn in Lilac, Hot Pink, Beige, Pink, Mint and Yellow

US B/1 (2.25-mm) hook

Tapestry needle

Polyester stuffing

Black embroidery floss

ABBREVIATIONS

rnd: round

ch: chain

sc: single crochet

1 inc: single crochet 2 stitches into the same stitch

1 dec: single crochet 2 stitches together

hdc: half double crochet

sl: slip stitch

st(s): stitch(es)

Approximate size for a finished Magical Unicorn Popsicle: 7 x 3 inches (18 x 8 cm)

Magical Unicorn Popsicle Pattern

POPSICLE

Using your Lilac yarn, ch 12.

RND 1: Starting in the second chain from the hook, 10 sc, 3 sc in the next st, turn around the corner and work in the loops on the other side of the chain, 9 sc, 1 inc (24 sc total).

RND 2: 1 inc, 9 sc, [1 inc] 3 times, 9 sc, [1 inc] 2 times (30 sc total)

RND 3: 1 inc, 11 sc, [1 inc] 4 times, 11 sc, [1 inc] 3 times (38 sc total)

RND 4–29: 38 sc (26 rounds, [38 sc in each round])

RND 30: In the back loops only, [1 dec] 3 times, 11 sc, [1 dec] 4 times, 11 sc, 1 dec (30 sc total)

RND 31: [3 sc, 1 dec] 6 times (24 sc total)

RND 32: [2 sc, 1 dec] 6 times (18 sc total)

Start stuffing, referring to the guide on page 11 if necessary.

RND 33: [1 sc, 1 dec] 6 times (12 sc total)

RND 34: [1 dec] 6 times (6 sc total)

Sew the hole together and fasten off all threads.

RASPBERRY SAUCE

Using your Hot Pink yarn, ch 12.

RND 1: Starting in the second chain from the hook, 10 sc, 3 sc in the next st, turn around the corner and work in the loops on the other side of the chain, 9 sc, 1 inc (24 sc total).

RND 2: 1 inc, 9 sc, [1 inc] 3 times, 9 sc, [1 inc] 2 times (30 sc total)

RND 3: 1 inc, 11 sc, [1 inc] 4 times, 11 sc, [1 inc] 3 times (38 sc total)

RND 4-11: 38 sc (8 rounds, [38 sc in each round])

Now you are going to crochet the sauce that's dripping down the popsicle.

1 sl in the next st

*Ch 6, starting in the second chain from the hook, 5 dc

Skip 1 st of round 11, 3 sl in round 11

Ch 5, starting in the second chain from the hook, 4 hdc

Skip 1 st, 3 sl, 4 hdc in the next st, 3 sc in the next st, 3 sl, 4 sc in the next st

Ch 4, starting in the second chain from the hook, 3 sc

Skip 1 st, 3 sl*

Repeat from * to * one more time.

1 sl in the last st.

Cut yarn but leave a long tail for sewing.

Pin the Raspberry Sauce on top of the Popsicle and sew it on.

EARS (MAKE 2)

Using your Lilac yarn, start with a magic ring.

RND 1: 6 sc into the magic ring (6 sc total)

RND 2: 6 sc (6 sc total)

RND 3: [1 inc] 6 times (12 sc total)

RND 4-6: 12 sc (3 rounds, [12 sc in each round])

RND 7: [1 sc, 1 dec] 4 times (8 sc total)

Finish with 1 sl.

Cut yarn but leave a long tail for sewing. Press the Ears flat with your hands, if necessary, and pin them to the Popsicle. Sew them on.

HORN

Using your Beige yarn, start with a magic ring.

RND 1: 6 sc into the magic ring (6 sc total)

RND 2: 6 sc (6 sc total)

RND 3: [1 sc, 1 inc] 3 times (9 sc total)

RND 4-7: 9 sc (4 rounds, [9 sc in each round])

Finish with 1 sl.

Cut yarn but leave a long tail for sewing.

Stuff the Horn just a little bit. Pin it to the top of the Popsicle and sew it on.

In this photo, the pink piece is what your rose should look like after Rows 1 and 2 but before you have sewed it together.

Roll the piece into a rose and sew it together through the center so it doesn't unroll.

Repeat with your Mint and Yellow yarns for a total of three roses.

ROSES (MAKE 3)

Using your Pink yarn, ch 8.

ROW 1: Starting in the second ch from the hook, 2 sc in each st, ch 1 (does not count as st), and turn (14 sc total).

ROW 2: 2 sc in each st (28 sc total)

Roll the piece into a rose and sew the piece together so it doesn't unroll.

Repeat with your Mint and Yellow yarns for a total of three roses.

Pin the Roses to the top of the Popsicle and sew them on.

Embroider black sleepy eyes and a mouth using your black embroidery floss.

CHEEKS (MAKE 2)

Using your Pink yarn, start with a magic ring.

RND 1: 6 sc into the magic ring (6 sc total)

Finish with 1 sl.

Cut yarn but leave a long tail for sewing. Pin the Cheeks to the Popsicle and sew them on.

TAIL

Using your Pink yarn, put your hook inside a stitch on the opposite side of the Popsicle from the embroidered face and pull the yarn through.

Ch 9, then 2 sc in second ch from hook and in each remaining ch (16 sc total)

Make 1 sl in the same st where you started, cut the yarn and secure it by weaving in your ends. Repeat this with your Mint and Yellow yarns so that you have three strands for the Tail.

STICK

Using your Beige yarn, start with a magic ring.

RND 1: 6 sc into the magic ring (6 sc total)

Start stuffing once you have made a few rounds, and keep stuffing a little at a time as you crochet more rounds.

RND 2–12: 6 sc (11 rounds, [6 sc in each round])

Finish with 1 sl.

Cut yarn but leave a long tail for sewing. Pin the Stick to the bottom of the Popsicle and sew it on.

Double the Fun Popsicle

What's better than one popsicle? Two popsicles! While making this, you'll crochet one popsicle at a time, then sew them together using sewing thread. It's an easy pattern, perfect for finishing in one afternoon, and you will have so much fun making it!

SKILL LEVEL: BEGINNER

MATERIALS

Light fingering weight yarn in Pink, Yellow, Mint, Sand and Purple
US B/1 (2.25-mm) hook
3 4-mm safety eyes
Tapestry needle
Black embroidery floss
Sewing thread
Small amounts of yarn in various yarn colors for sprinkles
Polyester stuffing

ABBREVIATIONS

rnd: round
ch: chain
sc: single crochet
1 inc: single crochet 2 stitches into the same stitch
1 dec: single crochet 2 stitches together
dc: double crochet
hdc: half double crochet
sl: slip stitch
st(s): stitch(es)

Approximate size for a finished Double the Fun Popsicle: 5 x 3 inches (13 x 8 cm)

Double the Fun Popsicle Pattern

POPSICLES (MAKE 2)

Using your Pink yarn, start with a magic ring.

RND 1: 6 sc into the magic ring (6 sc total)

RND 2: [1 inc] 6 times (12 sc total)

RND 3: [1 sc, 1 inc] 6 times (18 sc total)

RND 4: 1 sc, 1 inc [2 sc, 1 inc] 5 times, 1 sc (24 sc total)

RND 5: [3 sc, 1 inc] 6 times (30 sc total)

RND 6–13: 30 sc (8 rounds, [30 sc in each round])

Change to Yellow.

RND 14–21: 30 sc (8 rounds, [30 sc in each round])

Change to Mint.

RND 22–24: 30 sc (3 rounds, [30 sc in each round])

Now it's time to attach the safety eyes. On one of the Popsicles, attach a pair of safety eyes between rounds 17 and 18 with 5 st between them. Embroider a black mouth in the middle of round 19 using black embroidery floss.

On the second popsicle attach one safety eye between rounds 17 and 18.

Embroider a black mouth and a blinking eye using black embroidery floss. The blinking eye should be 4 st away from your safety eye.

RND 25–29: 30 sc (5 rounds, [30 sc in each round])

RND 30: In back loops only [3 sc, 1 dec] 6 times (24 sc total)

Start stuffing, referring to the guide on page 11.

RND 31: [2 sc, 1 dec] 6 times (18 sc total)

RND 32: [1 sc, 1 dec] 6 times (12 sc total)

RND 33: [1 dec] 6 times (6 sc total)

Sew the hole together and fasten off all threads.

Place the two Popsicles side-by-side and sew them together using sewing thread.

Embroider Pink cheeks on both popsicles using Pink yarn.

Embroider sprinkles all over the Pink section of your popsicles in different colors.

STICKS (MAKE 2)

Using your Sand yarn, start with a magic ring.

RND 1: 6 sc into the magic ring (6 sc total)

Start stuffing once you have made a few rounds, and keep stuffing a little at a time as you crochet more rounds.

RND 2–10: 6 sc (9 rounds, [6 sc in each round])

Finish with 1 sl.

Cut yarn but leave a long tail for sewing. Pin the Sticks to the bottom of the Popsicles and sew them on.

BOW

Using your Purple yarn, start with a magic ring, but don't pull it together.

Ch 3, 3 dc, ch 3, 1 sl, ch 3, 3 dc, ch 3, 1 sl into the ring

Pull the magic ring closed.

Cut the yarn but leave an 8-inch (20-cm)-long yarn tail. Pull the yarn tail around the middle of the Bow a couple of times until you think it looks good.

Sew the Bow onto the side of one of the Popsicles.

Bubbly Bunny Popsicle

Let this Bubbly Bunny Popsicle hop into your life and infuse your day with a bit of joy! When making this Bubbly Bunny Popsicle, you will start by making the base of the popsicle. You will then make the blueberry sauce that is placed over the popsicle and sewn on. Last, you'll add the ears, stick and, of course, a little carrot! It comes together quickly and can be turned into so many different animals if you just change up the ears!

SKILL LEVEL: BEGINNER

MATERIALS

Light fingering weight yarn in Light Blue, Purple, Orange, Green, Pink and Light Brown

US B/1 (2.25-mm) hook

Pair of 8-mm safety eyes

Tapestry needle

Black embroidery floss

Polyester stuffing

ABBREVIATIONS

rnd: round
ch: chain
sc: single crochet
1 inc: single crochet 2 stitches into the same stitch
1 dec: single crochet 2 stitches together
hdc: half double crochet
sl: slip stitch
st(s): stitch(es)

Approximate size for a finished Bubbly Bunny Popsicle: 7.5 x 2.5 inches (19 x 6 cm)

Bunny Popsicle Pattern

POPSICLE

Using your Light Blue yarn, ch 12.

RND 1: Starting in the second chain from the hook, 10 sc, 3 sc in the next st, turn around the corner and, working in the loops on the other side of the chain, 9 sc, 1 inc (24 sc total).

RND 2: 1 inc, 9 sc, [1 inc] 3 times, 9 sc, [1 inc] 2 times (30 sc total)

RND 3: 1 inc, 11 sc, [1 inc] 4 times, 11 sc, [1 inc] 3 times (38 sc total)

RND 4–29: 38 sc (26 rounds, [38 sc in each round])

Attach a pair of 8-mm safety eyes between rounds 15 and 16 with 7 st between them.

Embroider a black X as a mouth using black embroidery floss.

RND 30: In the back loops only, [1 dec] 3 times, 11 sc, [1 dec] 4 times, 11 sc, 1 dec (30 sc total)

RND 31: [3 sc, 1 dec] 6 times (24 sc total)

RND 32: [2 sc, 1 dec] 6 times (18 sc total)

Start stuffing, referring to the guide on page 11.

RND 33: [1 sc, 1 dec] 6 times (12 sc total)

RND 34: [1 dec] 6 times (6 sc total)

Sew the hole together and fasten off all threads.

BLUEBERRY SAUCE

Using your Purple yarn, ch 12.

RND 1: Starting in the second chain from the hook, 10 sc, 3 sc in the next st, turn around the corner and work in the loops on the other side of the chain, 9 sc, 1 inc (24 sc total).

RND 2: 1 inc, 9 sc, [1 inc] 3 times, 9 sc, [1 inc] 2 times (30 sc total)

RND 3: 1 inc, 11 sc, [1 inc] 4 times, 11 sc, [1 inc] 3 times (38 sc total)

RND 4–11: 38 sc (8 rounds, [38 sc in each round])

Now you are going to crochet the sauce that's dripping down the Popsicle.

1 sl in the next st

*Ch 6, starting in the second chain from the hook, 5 dc, skip 1 st of round 11, 3 sl in round 11

Ch 5, starting in the second chain from the hook, 4 hdc, skip 1 st, 3 sl, 4 hdc in the next st

3 sc in the next st, 3 sl, 4 sc in the next st

Ch 4, starting in the second chain from the hook, 3 sc, skip 1 st, 3 sl*

Repeat from * to * one more time.

1 sl in the last st

Cut yarn but leave a long tail for sewing. Pin the Blueberry Sauce on top of the Popsicle and sew it on.

EARS (MAKE 2)

Using your Light Blue yarn, start with a magic ring.

RND 1: 6 sc into the magic ring (6 sc total)

RND 2: [1 inc] 6 times (12 sc total)

RND 3–10: 12 sc (8 rounds, [12 sc in each round])

RND 11: [1 sc, 1 dec] 4 times (8 sc total)

Finish with 1 sl.

Cut yarn but leave a long tail for sewing. Press the Ears flat with your hands, if necessary, and pin them to the Popsicle. Sew them on.

CARROT

Using your Orange yarn, start with a magic ring.

RND 1: 6 sc into the magic ring (6 sc total)

RND 2: 6 sc (6 sc total)

RND 3: [1 sc, 1 inc] 3 times (9 sc total)

RND 4–6: 9 sc (3 rounds, [9 sc in each round])

Start stuffing, referring to the guide on page 11.

RND 7: In back loops only, [1 sc, 1 dec] 3 times (6 sc total)

Sew the hole together and fasten off all threads.

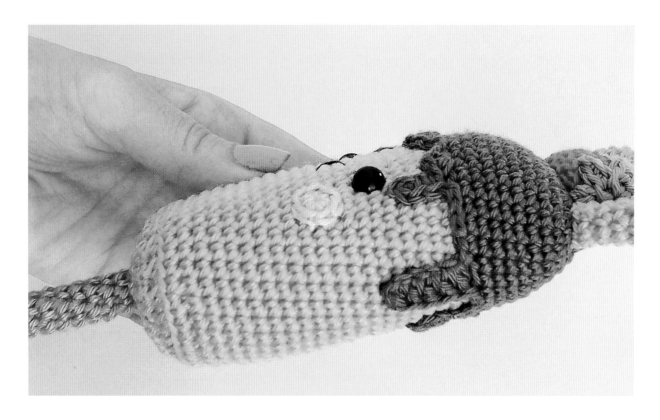

CARROT LEAVES

Using your Green yarn, start with a magic ring, but don't pull it together.

Ch 3, 1 sc in the second ch from the hook, 1 sc, 1 sl into the ring

Repeat from * to * 4 more times to create 5 leaves.

Pull the magic ring closed.

Cut yarn but leave a long tail for sewing. Sew the Leaves onto the Carrot.

Pin the Carrot on top of your Bubbly Bunny Popsicle and sew it on.

CHEEKS (MAKE 2)

Using your Pink yarn, start with a magic ring.

RND 1: 6 sc into the magic ring (6 sc total)

Finish with 1 sl.

Cut yarn but leave a long tail for sewing. Pin the Cheeks to the Popsicle and sew them on.

STICK

Using your Light Brown yarn, start with a magic ring.

RND 1: 6 sc into the magic ring (6 sc total)

Start stuffing once you have made a few rounds, and keep stuffing a little at a time as you crochet more rounds.

RND 2–12: 6 sc (11 rounds, [6 sc in each round])

Finish with 1 sl.

Cut yarn but leave a long tail for sewing. Pin the Stick to the bottom of the Popsicle and sew it on.

Three-Scoop Ice Cream Cone

You should never settle for just one scoop of ice cream, and in the case of this awesome amigurumi, you'll have three! You will start by making your cone. You'll then work your way up, crocheting and adding the bottom scoop, then the panda scoop and last, but not least, the unicorn scoop! This pattern has a lot of pieces and may take some time, but I promise you the delightful treat at the end will be worth it!

SKILL LEVEL: INTERMEDIATE

MATERIALS

Light fingering weight yarn in Sand, Hot Pink, Pink, White, Black, Lilac, Mint and Gray

US B/1 (2.25-mm) hook

3 6-mm safety eyes

Tapestry needle

Black embroidery floss

Polyester stuffing

White embroidery floss

Black sewing thread

ABBREVIATIONS

rnd: round

ch: chain

sc: single crochet

1 inc: single crochet 2 stitches into the same stitch

1 dec: single crochet 2 stitches together

dc: double crochet

hdc: half double crochet

sl: slip stitch

st(s): stitch(es)

Approximate size for a finished Three-Scoop Ice Cream Cone: 7.5 x 4 inches (19 x 10 cm)

Three-Scoop Ice Cream Cone Pattern

CONE

Using your Sand yarn, start with a magic ring.

RND 1: 6 sc into the magic ring (6 sc total)

RND 2: 6 sc (6 sc total)

RND 3: [1 inc] 6 times (12 sc total)

RND 4: 12 sc (12 sc total)

RND 5: [1 sc, 1 inc] 6 times (18 sc total)

RND 6–7: 18 sc (2 rounds, [18 sc in each round])

RND 8: [2 sc, 1 inc] 6 times (24 sc total)

RND 9–10: 24 sc (2 rounds, [24 sc in each round])

RND 11: [3 sc, 1 inc] 6 times (30 sc total)

RND 12–13: 30 sc (2 rounds, [30 sc in each round])

RND 14: [4 sc, 1 inc] 6 times (36 sc total)

RND 15–17: 36 sc (3 rounds, [36 sc in each round])

RND 18: [5 sc, 1 inc] 6 times (42 sc total)

RND 19–22: 42 sc (4 rounds, [42 sc in each round])

Cut yarn and fasten off all threads.

BOTTOM SCOOP

Using your Hot Pink yarn, start with a magic ring.

RND 1: 6 sc into the magic ring (6 sc total)

RND 2: [1 inc] 6 times (12 sc total)

RND 3: [1 sc, 1 inc] 6 times (18 sc total)

RND 4: 1 sc, 1 inc [2 sc, 1 inc] 5 times, 1 sc (24 sc total)

RND 5: [3 sc, 1 inc] 6 times (30 sc total)

RND 6: 2 sc, 1 inc [4 sc, 1 inc] 5 times, 2 sc (36 sc total)

RND 7: [5 sc, 1 inc] 6 times (42 sc total)

RND 8–15: 42 sc (8 rounds, [42 sc in each round])

RND 16: In front loops only, 4 hdc in each st

Finish with 1 sl.

Cut yarn but leave a long tail for sewing.

Attach a pair of 6-mm safety eyes between rounds 12 and 13 with 6 st between them.

Embroider a black mouth using black embroidery floss, and embroider pink cheeks using Pink yarn.

Sew the Bottom Scoop on top of the Cone. Don't forget to stuff it, referring to the guide on page 11.

PANDA SCOOP

Using your White yarn, start with a magic ring.

RND 1: 6 sc into the magic ring (6 sc total)

RND 2: [1 inc] 6 times (12 sc total)

RND 3: [1 sc, 1 inc] 6 times (18 sc total)

RND 4: 1 sc, 1 inc [2 sc, 1 inc] 5 times, 1 sc (24 sc total)

RND 5: [3 sc, 1 inc] 6 times (30 sc total)

RND 6: 2 sc, 1 inc [4 sc, 1 inc] 5 times, 2 sc (36 sc total)

RND 7: [5 sc, 1 inc] 6 times (42 sc total)

RND 8–15: 42 sc (8 rounds, [42 sc in each round])

RND 16: In front loops only, *5 hdc, skip 1 st, 1 sl, skip 1 st*

Repeat from * to * for the entire round, ending after 5 hdc on the final repeat.

Finish with 1 sl.

Cut yarn but leave a long tail for sewing.

Sew the Panda Scoop on top of the Bottom Scoop. Don't forget to stuff it, referring to the guide on page 11.

PANDA EYES (MAKE 2)

Using your Black yarn, start with a magic ring.

RND 1: 6 sc into the magic ring (6 sc total)

RND 2: [1 inc] 6 times (12 sc total)

Finish with 1 sl.

Cut yarn and fasten off all threads.

Embroider white sleepy eyes using white embroidery floss.

Pin the Eyes to the Panda Scoop and sew them on using black sewing thread.

Embroider a pink nose using your Pink yarn, then embroider a mouth using your black embroidery thread.

PANDA EARS (MAKE 2)

Using your Black yarn, start with a magic ring.

RND 1: 6 sc into the magic ring (6 sc total)

RND 2: [1 inc] 6 times (12 sc total)

RND 3–5: 12 sc (3 rounds, [12 sc in each round])

RND 6: [1 sc, 1 dec] 4 times (8 sc total)

Finish with 1 sl.

Cut yarn but leave a long tail for sewing.

Wait until you have attached the Unicorn Scoop before sewing on the Panda Ears.

UNICORN SCOOP

Using your Lilac yarn, start with a magic ring.

RND 1: 6 sc into the magic ring (6 sc total)

RND 2: [1 inc] 6 times (12 sc total)

RND 3: [1 sc, 1 inc] 6 times (18 sc total)

RND 4: 1 sc, 1 inc [2 sc, 1 inc] 5 times, 1 sc (24 sc total)

RND 5: [3 sc, 1 inc] 6 times (30 sc total)

RND 6: 2 sc, 1 inc [4 sc, 1 inc] 5 times, 2 sc (36 sc total)

RND 7: [5 sc, 1 inc] 6 times (42 sc total)

RND 8–15: 42 sc (8 rounds, [42 sc in each round])

RND 16: In front loops only, *5 hdc, skip 1 st, 1 sl, skip 1 st*

Repeat from * to * for the entire round, ending after 5 hdc on the final repeat.

Finish with 1 sl.

Cut yarn but leave a long tail for sewing.

Embroider a black mouth using black embroidery floss in the middle of round 13.

Attach one 6-mm safety eye between rounds 12 and 13.

Embroider a blinking eye 6 st away from the safety eye using black embroidery floss and pink cheeks using Pink yarn.

Sew the Unicorn Scoop on top of the Panda Scoop. Don't forget to stuff it, referring to the guide on page 11. Pin the Panda Ears to the Panda Scoop and sew them on.

FROSTING

Using your Mint yarn, start with a magic ring.

RND 1: 6 sc into the magic ring (6 sc total)

RND 2: [1 inc] 6 times (12 sc total)

RND 3: [1 sc, 1 inc] 6 times (18 sc total)

RND 4: 1 sc, 1 inc [2 sc, 1 inc] 5 times, 1 sc (24 sc total)

RND 5: [3 sc, 1 inc] 6 times (30 sc total)

RND 6: 2 sc, 1 inc [4 sc, 1 inc] 5 times, 2 sc (36 sc total)

RND 7: [5 sc, 1 inc] 6 times (42 sc total)

Now you are going to crochet the frosting that's dripping down the Unicorn Scoop.

Ch 4, starting in the second ch from the hook, 3 hdc

Skip 1 st of round 7, 3 sl in round 7

Ch 6, starting in the second ch from the hook, 5 hdc

Skip 1 st, 3 sl

Ch 5, starting in the second ch from the hook, 4 hdc

Skip 1 st, 3 sl

Ch 3, starting in the second ch from the hook, 2 hdc

Skip 1 st, 3 sl, 4 hdc in the same st, 3 sl

Ch 4, starting in the second ch from the hook, 3 hdc

Skip 1 st, 3 sl

Ch 6, starting in the second ch from the hook, 5 hdc

Skip 1 st, 3 sl

Ch 3, starting in the second ch from the hook, 2 hdc

Skip 1 st, 3 sl, 4 hdc in the same st, 3 sl

Ch 4, starting in the second ch from the hook, 3 hdc

Skip 1 st, 4 sl

Cut yarn but leave a long tail for sewing.

Pin the Frosting on top of the Unicorn Scoop and sew it on.

UNICORN EARS (MAKE 2)

Using your Lilac yarn, start with a magic ring.

RND 1: 6 sc into the magic ring (6 sc total)

RND 2: 6 sc (6 sc total)

RND 3: [1 inc] 6 times (12 sc total)

RND 4–5: 12 sc (2 rounds, [12 sc in each round])

RND 6: [1 sc, 1 dec] 4 times (8 sc total)

Finish with 1 sl.

Cut yarn but leave a long tail for sewing. Press the Ears flat with your hands, if necessary, and pin them to the Unicorn Scoop. Sew them on.

UNICORN HORN

Using your Gray yarn, start with a magic ring.

RND 1: 6 sc into the magic ring (6 sc total)

RND 2: 6 sc (6 sc total)

RND 3: [1 sc, 1 inc] 3 times (9 sc total)

RND 4–5: 9 sc (2 rounds, [9 sc in each round])

Finish with 1 sl.

Cut yarn but leave a long tail for sewing.

Stuff the Horn just a little bit. Pin it to the top of the Unicorn Scoop and sew it on.

Kitty Sundae

I am a huge cat lover—some may even call me a crazy cat lady! Combine that with my sweet tooth and a sundae pattern with a cute kitty cat face was a given. This Kitty Sundae is made in separate pieces that you sew together. My favorite piece is the frosting on top, and I like to embroider lots of sprinkles all over to make it look extra yummy! The Kitty Sundae is a fun make and can easily be turned into a different animal if you let your imagination run wild. Maybe you are more of a dog person? Have fun with it, and tailor it to your favorite creature if you'd like!

SKILL LEVEL: INTERMEDIATE

MATERIALS

Light fingering weight yarn in Sand, Gray, Pink, Mint, Red and Green

Small amounts of various yarn colors for sprinkles

US B/1 (2.25-mm) hook

Tapestry needle

A pair of 7-mm safety eyes

Black embroidery floss

Polyester stuffing

ABBREVIATIONS

rnd: round

ch: chain

sc: single crochet

1 inc: single crochet 2 stitches into the same stitch

1 dec: single crochet 2 stitches together

dc: double crochet

hdc: half double crochet

sl: slip stitch

st(s): stitch(es)

Approximate size for a finished Kitty Sundae: 5 x 4 inches (13 x 10 cm)

Kitty Sundae Pattern

CONE

Using your Sand yarn, start with a magic ring.

RND 1: 6 sc into the magic ring (6 sc total)

RND 2: [1 inc] 6 times (12 sc total)

RND 3: [1 sc, 1 inc] 6 times (18 sc total)

RND 4: 1 sc, 1 inc [2 sc, 1 inc] 5 times, 1 sc (24 sc total)

RND 5: [3 sc, 1 inc] 6 times (30 sc total)

RND 6: In back loops only, 30 sc (30 sc)

RND 7–16: 30 sc (10 rounds, [30 sc in each round])

RND 17: In back loops only, 30 sc (30 sc)

RND 18: 2 sc, 1 inc [4 sc, 1 inc] 5 times, 2 sc (36 sc total)

RND 19: [5 sc, 1 inc] 6 times (42 sc total)

RND 20: 3 sc, 1 inc [6 sc, 1 inc] 5 times, 3 sc (48 sc total)

RND 21–23: 48 sc (3 rounds, [48 sc in each round])

1 sl in the next st

Turn the Cone around so that you have the opening against you. You will crochet in the front loops of this round so that the back loops are visible when you turn to the right side.

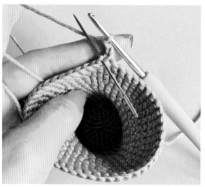

This is what your piece should look like after Rnd 23.

Turn the Cone around so that you have the opening against you. Ch 2.

Crochet 1 dc in each st for the entire rnd.

Finish with 1 sl.

Cut your yarn and fasten off all threads.

RND 24: In front loops only ch 2 (does not count as st), *1 dc in each st*

Repeat from * to * for entire round.

Finish with 1 sl.

Cut yarn and fasten off all threads.

ICE CREAM

Using your Gray yarn, start with a magic ring.

RND 1: 6 sc into the magic ring (6 sc total)

RND 2: [1 inc] 6 times (12 sc total)

RND 3: [1 sc, 1 inc] 6 times (18 sc total)

RND 4: 1 sc, 1 inc [2 sc, 1 inc] 5 times, 1 sc (24 sc total)

RND 5: [3 sc, 1 inc] 6 times (30 sc total)

RND 6: 2 sc, 1 inc [4 sc, 1 inc] 5 times, 2 sc (36 sc total)

RND 7: [5 sc, 1 inc] 6 times (42 sc total)

RND 8: 3 sc, 1 inc [6 sc, 1 inc] 5 times, 3 sc (48 sc total)

RND 9–17: 48 sc (9 rounds, [48 sc in each round])

RND 18: In front loops only, *5 hdc in the next stitch, skip 1 st, 1 sl, skip 1 st*

Repeat from * to * for the entire round.

Cut yarn but leave a long tail for sewing.

Attach the 7-mm safety eyes between rounds 11 and 12 with 7 sc between them.

Embroider a nose using black embroidery floss and Pink yarn

Sew the Ice Cream on top of the Cone. Don't forget to stuff it, referring to the guide on page 11.

FROSTING

Using your Mint yarn, start with a magic ring.

RND 1: 6 sc into the magic ring (6 sc total)

RND 2: [1 inc] 6 times (12 sc total)

RND 3: [1 sc, 1 inc] 6 times (18 sc total)

RND 4: 1 sc, 1 inc [2 sc, 1 inc] 5 times, 1 sc (24 sc total)

RND 5: [3 sc, 1 inc] 6 times (30 sc total)

RND 6: 2 sc, 1 inc [4 sc, 1 inc] 5 times, 2 sc (36 sc total)

RND 7: [5 sc, 1 inc] 6 times (42 sc total)

RND 8: *4 dc in the next st, skip 1 st, 1 sl, skip 1 st, 4 sc in the next st, skip 1 st*

Repeat from * to * for the entire round.

Cut your yarn but leave a long tail for sewing.

Pin the Frosting on top of the Ice Cream and sew it on.

Embroider sprinkles in different colors.

EARS (MAKE 2)

Using your Gray yarn, start with a magic ring.

RND 1: 6 sc into the magic ring (6 sc total)

RND 2: 6 sc (6 sc total)

RND 3: [1 inc] 6 times (12 sc total)

RND 4–5: 12 sc (2 rounds, [12 sc in each round])

RND 6: [2 sc, 1 dec] 3 times (9 sc total)

Finish with 1 sl.

Cut yarn but leave a long tail for sewing. Press the Ears flat with your hands, if necessary, and pin them to the Ice Cream. Sew them on.

CHEEKS (MAKE 2)

Using your Pink yarn, start with a magic ring.

RND 1: 6 sc into the magic ring (6 sc total)

Finish with 1 sl.

Cut yarn but leave a long tail for sewing. Pin the Cheeks to the Ice Cream and sew them on.

Embroider whiskers using your black embroidery floss.

STRAWBERRY

Using your Red yarn, start with a magic ring.

RND 1: 6 sc into the magic ring

RND 2: 6 sc (6 sc total)

RND 3: [1 inc] 6 times (12 sc total)

RND 4–5: 12 sc (2 rounds, [12 sc in each round])

Start stuffing your Strawberry.

RND 6: In back loops only, [1 dec] 6 times (6 sc total)

Sew the hole together and fasten off.

STRAWBERRY LEAVES

Using your Green yarn, start with a magic ring, but don't pull it together.

Ch 3, 1 sc in the second ch from the hook, 1 sc, 1 sl into the ring

Repeat from * to * 4 more times to create 5 leaves.

Pull the magic ring closed.

Cut your yarn but leave a long tail for sewing. Sew the Leaves onto the Strawberry.

Pin the Strawberry on top of your Kitty Sundae and sew it on.

One in a Melon

FUN, FRUITY PROJECTS FOR EVERYONE

Whether you like strawberries best or if watermelons are more your thing, you're sure to find a pattern in this chapter that you will enjoy making! Crochet your way through five playful projects designed to evoke the fresh flavors of spring and summer and have an adorable bowl of amigurumi fruit once you're all done. For extra cuteness, each little design has added legs and arms.

In this chapter, you will find four beginner-friendly patterns and one pattern that might be a little bit more challenging. The Adorable Avocado (page 51) has a slightly different construction from the rest of the designs, so its skill level is intermediate. But don't let that frighten you! The pattern also includes some useful photos to walk you through any tricky steps. The Wonderful Watermelon (page 47) is another favorite of mine, and it's not just because it's super cute— it can be turned into several different fruits! Make it with orange yarn, and you'll have a juicy orange slice, use green and you'll have a lime or use yellow and you'll have a huge lemon. You can have a fresh squeeze any day of the year!

Sweet Strawberry

This sweet and delicious strawberry is crocheted starting at the bottom, then you'll work your way toward the top. The legs, arms and leaf are sewn onto the strawberry. Feel free to switch up the expression to a sassy or surprised strawberry, and, most important, have fun with it!

SKILL LEVEL: BEGINNER

MATERIALS

Light fingering weight yarn in Red, Green and Pink
US B/1 (2.25-mm) hook
A pair of 6-mm safety eyes
Tapestry needle
Black embroidery floss
Polyester stuffing

ABBREVIATIONS

rnd: round
ch: chain
sc: single crochet
1 inc: single crochet 2 stitches into the same stitch
1 dec: single crochet 2 stitches together
hdc: half double crochet
sl: slip stitch
st(s): stitch(es)

Approximate size for a finished Sweet Strawberry:
4 x 3 inches (10 x 8 cm)

Sweet Strawberry Pattern

STRAWBERRY

Using your Red yarn, start with a magic ring.

RND 1: 6 sc into the magic ring (6 sc total)

RND 2: [1 inc] 6 times (12 sc total)

RND 3: [1 sc, 1 inc] 6 times (18 sc total)

RND 4: 1 sc, 1 inc [2 sc, 1 inc] 5 times, 1 sc (24 sc total)

RND 5: [3 sc, 1 inc] 6 times (30 sc total)

RND 6: 2 sc, 1 inc [4 sc, 1 inc] 5 times, 2 sc (36 sc total)

RND 7: 36 sc (36 sc total)

RND 8: [5 sc, 1 inc] 6 times (42 sc total)

RND 9: 42 sc (42 sc total)

RND 10: 3 sc, 1 inc [6 sc, 1 inc] 5 times, 3 sc (48 sc total)

RND 11: 48 sc (48 sc total)

RND 12: [7 sc, 1 inc] 6 times (54 sc total)

RND 13–21: 54 sc (9 rounds, [54 sc in each round])

RND 22: [7 sc, 1 dec] 6 times (48 sc total)

RND 23: 3 sc, 1 dec [6 sc, 1 dec] 5 times, 3 sc (42 sc total)

Now it's time to attach the safety eyes.

Attach a pair of eyes between rounds 15 and 16 with 7 st between them.

Embroider a black mouth using black embroidery floss in the middle of round 14.

RND 24: [5 sc, 1 dec] 6 times (36 sc total)

RND 25: 2 sc, 1 dec [4 sc, 1 dec] 5 times, 2 sc (30 sc total)

Start stuffing, referring to the guide on page 11.

RND 26: [3 sc, 1 dec] 6 times (24 sc total)

RND 27: 1 sc, 1 dec [2 sc, 1 dec] 5 times (18 sc total)

RND 28: [1 sc, 1 dec] 6 times (12 sc total)

RND 29: [1 dec] 6 times (6 sc total)

Cut yarn and fasten off all threads.

LEAF

Using your Green yarn, start with a magic ring.

RND 1: 6 sc into the magic ring (6 sc total)

RND 2: [1 inc] 6 times (12 sc total)

RND 3: [1 sc, 1 inc] 6 times (18 sc total)

RND 4: 1 sc, 1 inc [2 sc, 1 inc] 5 times, 1 sc (24 sc total)

RND 5: [3 sc, 1 inc] 6 times (30 sc total)

RND 6: 2 sc, 1 inc [4 sc, 1 inc] 5 times, 2 sc (36 sc total)

RND 7: [5 sc, 1 inc] 6 times (42 sc total)

*Ch 6, starting in the second ch from the hook, 5 hdc, skip next st of round 7, 3 sl into round 7

Ch 5, starting in the second ch from the hook, 4 hdc, skip next st of round 7, 3 sl into round 7*

Repeat from * to * 4 more times.

Finish with 2 sl.

Cut yarn and leave a long tail for sewing.

Pin the Leaf to the top of the Strawberry and sew it on.

STALK

Using your Green yarn, ch 6.

RND 1: Starting in the second ch from the hook, 5 sc (5 sc total)

Cut yarn and leave a long tail for sewing.

Pin the Stalk on top of the Leaf and sew it on.

LEGS (MAKE 2)

Using your Red yarn, start with a magic ring.

RND 1: 6 sc into the magic ring (6 sc total)

RND 2: [1 inc] 6 times (12 sc total)

RND 3–6: 12 sc (4 rounds, [12 sc in each round])

Finish with 1 sl.

Stuff the Legs. Pin the Legs to the Strawberry and sew them on.

ARMS (MAKE 2)

Using your Red yarn, start with a magic ring.

RND 1: 6 sc into the magic ring (6 sc total)

RND 2–7: 6 sc (6 rounds, [6 sc in each round])

Finish with 1 sl.

Pin the Arms to the Strawberry and sew them on.

CHEEKS (MAKE 2)

Using your Pink yarn, start with a magic ring.

RND 1: 6 sc into the magic ring (6 sc total)

Finish with 1 sl.

Cut yarn but leave a long tail for sewing. Pin the Cheeks to the Strawberry and sew them on.

Precious Pear

This precious little pear is made starting at the bottom and working to the top. It works up quite fast and easily—you could say it's the "pearfect" project for a summer afternoon! A lilac pear is not something you see every day, but that's one of the best things about amigurumi: You can make your creations in whatever color you like. Why not make a pink pear, too, so they can make the pearfect pair together?

SKILL LEVEL: BEGINNER

MATERIALS

Light fingering weight yarn in Lilac, Brown, Green and Pink
US B/1 (2.25-mm) hook
A pair of 6-mm safety eyes
Tapestry needle
Black embroidery floss
Polyester stuffing

ABBREVIATIONS

rnd: round
ch: chain
sc: single crochet
1 inc: single crochet 2 stitches into the same stitch
1 dec: single crochet 2 stitches together
dc: double crochet
hdc: half double crochet
sl: slip stitch
st(s): stitch(es)

Approximate size for a finished Precious Pear:
4.7 x 2.7 inches (12 x 7 cm)

Precious Pear Pattern

PEAR

Using your Lilac yarn, start with a magic ring.

RND 1: 6 sc into the magic ring (6 sc total)

RND 2: [1 inc] 6 times (12 sc total)

RND 3: [1 sc, 1 inc] 6 times (18 sc total)

RND 4: 1 sc, 1 inc [2 sc, 1 inc] 5 times, 1 sc (24 sc total)

RND 5: [3 sc, 1 inc] 6 times (30 sc total)

RND 6: 2 sc, 1 inc [4 sc, 1 inc] 5 times, 2 sc (36 sc total)

RND 7: [5 sc, 1 inc] 6 times (42 sc total)

RND 8: 3 sc, 1 inc [6 sc, 1 inc] 5 times, 3 sc (48 sc total)

RND 9: [7 sc, 1 inc] 6 times (54 sc total)

RND 10–16: 54 sc (7 rounds, [54 sc in each round])

RND 17: [7 sc, 1 dec] 6 times (48 sc total)

RND 18: 3 sc, 1 dec [6 sc, 1 dec] 5 times, 3 sc (42 sc total)

RND 19: [5 sc, 1 dec] 6 times (36 sc total)

RND 20–25: 36 sc (6 rounds, [36 sc in each round])

RND 26: 2 sc, 1 dec [4 sc, 1 dec] 5 times, 2 sc (30 sc total)

Now it's time to attach the safety eyes.

Attach a pair of 6-mm safety eyes between rounds 22 and 23, approximately 5 st apart.

Embroider a black mouth using black embroidery floss in the middle of round 21.

RND 27–32: 30 sc (6 rounds, [30 sc in each round])

RND 33: [3 sc, 1 dec] 6 times (24 sc total)

Start stuffing, referring to the guide on page 11.

RND 34: 1 sc, 1 dec [2 sc, 1 dec] 5 times, 1 sc (18 sc total)

RND 35: 18 sc (18 sc total)

RND 36: [1 sc, 1 dec] 6 times (12 sc total)

RND 37: [1 dec] 6 times (6 sc total)

Cut yarn and fasten off all threads.

STEM

Using your Brown yarn, ch 6.

RND 1: Starting in the second ch from the hook, 5 sc (5 sc total)

Cut yarn and leave a long tail for sewing.

Pin the Stem on top of the Pear and sew it on.

LEAF

Using your Green yarn, ch 7.

RND 1: Starting in the second ch from the hook, 1 sc, 1 hdc, 3 dc, 3 sc in the next ch, turn around the corner and work in the loops on the other side of the chain, 3 dc, 1 hdc, 1 sc.

Finish with 1 sl.

Cut yarn but leave a long tail for sewing.

Pin the Leaf to the Pear and sew it on.

CHEEKS (MAKE 2)

Using your Pink yarn, start with a magic ring.

RND 1: 6 sc into the magic ring (6 sc total)

Finish with 1 sl.

Cut yarn but leave a long tail for sewing. Pin the Cheeks to the Pear and sew them on.

LEGS (MAKE 2)

Using your Brown yarn, ch 4.

RND 1: Starting in the second ch from the hook, 2 sc, 3 sc in the next ch, turn around the corner and work in the loops on the other side of the chain, 1 sc, 2 sc in the next ch (8 sc total).

RND 2: 1 inc, 1 sc, [1 inc] 3 times, 1 sc, 1 inc, 1 sc (13 sc total)

RND 3: 5 sc, 3 hdc, 5 sc (13 st total)

RND 4: 4 sc, 1 dec, 2 sc, 1 dec, 3 sc (11 sc total)

RND 5: [1 dec] 5 times, 1 sc (6 sc total)

Stuff the feet.

RND 6–9: 6 sc (4 rounds, [6 sc in each round])

Cut yarn but leave a long tail for sewing.

Pin the Legs to the Pear and sew them on.

ARMS (MAKE 2)

Using your Brown yarn, start with a magic ring.

RND 1: 6 sc into the magic ring (6 sc total)

RND 2–6: 6 sc (5 rounds, [6 sc in each round])

Finish with 1 sl.

Cut yarn but leave a long tail for sewing. You do not need to stuff the arms. Pin the Arms to the Pear and sew them on.

Lovely Lemon

This lemon sure is lovely to make. You only need a small amount of yarn, and you can easily make one or two in an afternoon. You will first crochet the lemon, then make the arms and legs before sewing them onto the body. Play with the facial expression if you like; why not make it with sleepy eyes or embroider a sour face instead?

SKILL LEVEL: BEGINNER

MATERIALS

Light fingering weight yarn in Green,
Yellow, Pink and Brown
US B/1 (2.25-mm) hook
A pair of 6-mm safety eyes
Tapestry needle
Black embroidery floss
Polyester stuffing

ABBREVIATIONS

rnd: round
ch: chain
sc: single crochet
1 inc: single crochet 2 stitches into
the same stitch
1 dec: single crochet 2 stitches together
dc: double crochet
hdc: half double crochet
sl: slip stitch
st(s): stitch(es)

Approximate size for a finished Lovely
Lemon: 3 x 4 inches (8 x 10 cm)

Lovely Lemon Pattern

LEMON

Using your Green yarn, start with a magic ring.

RND 1: 6 sc into the ring (6 sc total)

RND 2: 6 sc (6 sc total)

Change to Yellow.

RND 3: [1 inc] 6 times (12 sc total)

RND 4: 12 sc (12 sc total)

RND 5: [1 sc, 1 inc] 6 times (18 sc total)

RND 6: [2 sc, 1 inc] 6 times (24 sc total)

RND 7: 24 sc (24 sc total)

RND 8: [3 sc, 1 inc] 6 times (30 sc total)

RND 9: [4 sc, 1 inc] 6 times (36 sc total)

RND 10: 36 sc (36 sc total)

RND 11: [5 sc, 1 inc] 6 times (42 sc total)

RND 12: [6 sc, 1 inc] 6 times (48 sc total)

RND 13–22: 48 sc (10 rounds, [48 sc in each round])

RND 23: [6 sc, 1 dec] 6 times (42 sc total)

RND 24: [5 sc, 1 dec] 6 times (36 sc total)

CHEEKS (MAKE 2)

Using your Pink yarn, start with a magic ring.

RND 1: 6 sc into the magic ring (6 sc total)

Finish with 1 sl.

Cut yarn but leave a long tail for sewing. Pin the Cheeks to the Lemon and sew them on.

LEAVES (MAKE 2)

Using your Green yarn, ch 8.

RND 1: Starting in the second ch from the hook, 1 sc, 1 hdc, 4 dc, 3 sc in the next ch, turn around the corner and work in the loops on the other side of the ch, 4 dc, 1 hdc, 1 sc.

Finish with 1 sl.

Cut yarn but leave a long tail for sewing.

Pin the Leaves to the Lemon and sew them on.

LEGS (MAKE 2)

Using your Brown yarn, ch 4.

RND 1: Starting in the second ch from the hook, 2 sc, 3 sc in the next ch, turn around the corner and work in the loops on the other side of the chain, 1 sc, 2 sc in the next ch (8 sc total).

RND 2: 1 inc, 1 sc, [1 inc] 3 times, 1 sc, 1 inc, 1 sc (13 sc total)

RND 3: 5 sc, 3 hdc, 5 sc (13 st total)

RND 4: 4 sc, 1 dec, 2 sc, 1 dec, 3 sc (11 sc total)

RND 5: [1 dec] 5 times, 1 sc (6 sc total)

Stuff the feet.

RND 6–8: 6 sc (3 rounds, [6 sc in each round])

Cut yarn but leave a long tail for sewing.

Pin the Legs to the Lemon and sew them on.

RND 25: 36 sc (36 sc total)

RND 26: [4 sc, 1 dec] 6 times (30 sc total)

RND 27: 30 sc (30 sc total)

Now it's time to attach the safety eyes and embroider a mouth.

Attach one 6-mm safety eye between rounds 13 and 14. Attach the second eye between rounds 21 and 22. Try to keep the eyes as even as possible. Embroider a black mouth using black embroidery floss.

RND 28: [3 sc, 1 dec] 6 times (24 sc total)

Start stuffing, referring to the guide on page 11.

RND 29: [2 sc, 1 dec] 6 times (18 sc total)

RND 30: 18 sc (18 sc total)

RND 31: [1 sc, 1 dec] 6 times (12 sc total)

RND 32: 12 sc (12 sc total)

RND 33: [1 dec] 6 times (6 sc total)

Cut yarn and fasten off all threads.

Wonderful Watermelon

This watermelon is made in one round piece and one edge piece that gives the watermelon its depth and texture. It works up quickly and is super fun to make! No matter the season you're in, let this little guy give you a fresh burst of summer vibes!

SKILL LEVEL: BEGINNER

MATERIALS

Light fingering weight yarn in Light Red, White, Green, Dark Green, Pink and Brown
US B/1 (2.25-mm) hook
Tapestry needle
Black embroidery floss
A pair of 6-mm safety eyes
Polyester stuffing

ABBREVIATIONS

rnd: round
ch: chain
sc: single crochet
1 inc: single crochet 2 stitches into the same stitch
1 dec: single crochet 2 stitches together
hdc: half double crochet
sl: slip stitch
st(s): stitch(es)

Approximate size for a finished Wonderful Watermelon: 4.7 x 2.7 inches (12 x 7 cm)

Wonderful Watermelon Pattern

WATERMELON

Using your Light Red yarn, start with a magic ring.

RND 1: 6 sc into the ring (6 sc total)

RND 2: [1 inc] 6 times (12 sc total)

RND 3: [1 sc, 1 inc] 6 times (18 sc total)

RND 4: 1 sc, 1 inc [2 sc, 1 inc] 5 times, 1 sc (24 sc total)

RND 5: [3 sc, 1 inc] 6 times (30 sc total)

RND 6: 2 sc, 1 inc [4 sc, 1 inc] 5 times, 2 sc (36 sc total)

RND 7: [5 sc, 1 inc] 6 times (42 sc total)

RND 8: 3 sc, 1 inc [6 sc, 1 inc] 5 times, 3 sc (48 sc total)

RND 9: [7 sc, 1 inc] 6 times (54 sc total)

RND 10: 4 sc, 1 inc [8 sc, 1 inc] 5 times, 4 sc (60 sc total)

RND 11: [9 sc, 1 inc] 6 times (66 sc total)

RND 12: 5 sc, 1 inc [10 sc, 1 inc] 5 times, 5 sc (72 sc total)

RND 13: [11 sc, 1 inc] 6 times (78 sc total)

Change to White.

RND 14: 6 sc, 1 inc [12 sc, 1 inc] 5 times, 6 sc (84 sc total)

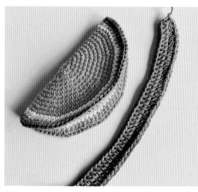
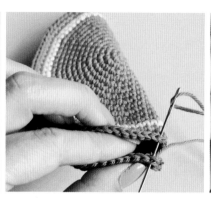

This is what your watermelon and green edge pieces should look like before being sewn together.

Sew the green edge onto the bottom, starting on the upper corner of the watermelon.

Continue to sew the pieces together, until you have about 2 inches (5 cm) left, then start stuffing.

Change to Green.

RND 15: [13 sc, 1 inc] 6 times (90 sc total)

Change to Dark Green.

RND 16: 7 sc, 1 inc [14 sc, 1 inc] 5 times, 7 sc (96 sc total)

Finish with 3 sl. Cut yarn and fasten off all threads.

Fold the piece.

Embroider a black mouth using black embroidery floss in the middle of round 10. Attach a pair of 6-mm safety eyes between rounds 9 and 10 with approximately 7 st between them.

GREEN EDGE

Using your Green yarn, ch 47.

RND 1: Starting in the second ch from the hook, 45 hdc, 3 hdc in the next st, turn around the corner and work in the loops on the other side of the ch, 44 hdc, 1 inc.

Finish with 1 sl in the first hdc.

Cut yarn but leave a long tail for sewing.

Take the Green Edge and place it along the bottom of your Watermelon.

Sew the Green Edge onto the bottom. (I prefer to start on the upper side on the backside of the Watermelon.)

When you have about 2 inches (5 cm) left, start stuffing. Don't stuff it too hard and make sure to flatten it as you are stuffing so it makes a nice, flat watermelon slice shape.

CHEEKS (MAKE 2)

Using your Pink yarn, start with a magic ring.

RND 1: 6 sc into the magic ring (6 sc total)

Finish with 1 sl.

Cut yarn but leave a long tail for sewing. Pin the Cheeks to the Watermelon and sew them on.

LEGS (MAKE 2)

Using your Brown yarn, ch 4.

RND 1: Starting in the second ch from the hook, 2 sc, 3 sc in the next ch, turn around the corner and work in the loops on the other side of the ch, 1 sc, 2 sc in the next ch (8 sc total).

RND 2: 1 inc, 1 sc, [1 inc] 3 times, 1 sc, 1 inc, 1 sc (13 sc total)

RND 3: 5 sc, 3 hdc, 5 sc (13 st total)

RND 4: 4 sc, 1 dec, 2 sc, 1 dec, 3 sc (11 sc total)

RND 5: [1 dec] 5 times, 1 sc (6 sc total)

Stuff the feet.

RND 6–8: 6 sc (3 rounds, [6 sc in each round])

Cut yarn but leave a long tail for sewing.

Pin the Legs to the Watermelon and sew them on.

Embroider black seeds using your black embroidery floss.

Adorable Avocado

This chubby and adorable avocado is made in two pieces that are then crocheted together. The arms and legs are made separately and then sewn on. While the construction is a little different from the rest of the fruits in this chapter, don't feel intimidated. This is still a rather quick make and you will have a lot of fun! You may not be able to put this avocado on toast, but it's so cute, so why would you even want to?

SKILL LEVEL: INTERMEDIATE

MATERIALS

Light fingering weight yarn in Brown, Green, Dark Green and Pink

US B/1 (2.25-mm) hook

A pair of 5-mm safety eyes

Tapestry needle

Black embroidery floss

Polyester stuffing

ABBREVIATIONS

rnd: round

ch: chain

sc: single crochet

1 inc: single crochet 2 stitches into the same stitch

1 dec: single crochet 2 stitches together

hdc: half double crochet

sl: slip stitch

st(s): stitch(es)

Approximate size for a finished Adorable Avocado: 4.3 x 3.5 inches (11 x 9 cm)

Adorable Avocado Pattern

AVOCADO FRONT

Using your Brown yarn, start with a magic ring.

RND 1: 5 sc into the magic ring (5 sc total)

RND 2: [1 inc] 5 times (10 sc total)

RND 3: [1 sc, 1 inc] 5 times (15 sc total)

RND 4: [2 sc, 1 inc] 5 times (20 sc total)

RND 5: [3 sc, 1 inc] 5 times (30 sc total)

RND 6–7: 30 sc (2 rounds, [30 sc total])

Change to Green.

RND 8: [4 sc, 1 inc] 5 times (35 sc total)

RND 9: [5 sc, 1 inc] 5 times (40 sc total)

RND 10: [6 sc, 1 inc] 5 times (45 sc total)

RND 11: [7 sc, 1 inc] 5 times (50 sc total)

RND 12: [8 sc, 1 inc] 5 times (55 sc total)

RND 13: [9 sc, 1 inc] 5 times (60 sc total)

ROW 14: 1 inc, 7 sc, 1 inc, ch 1 (does not count as st throughout), and turn leaving the remaining sts unworked (11 sc total)

Now work back and forth in rows for the rest of the piece.

ROW 15–17: 11 sc, ch 1 and turn (3 rows, [11 sc in each row])

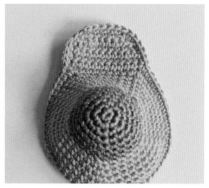

This is what your piece should look like after Rnd 13.

After you have worked back and forth for Rows 14 to 20, your piece should look like this.

After you have sc around the whole piece, it should look like this.

This is what the back and front pieces of the avocado should look like, before being sewn together.

Sc the two pieces together, working 1 sc through both layers in each st to join, using your Dark Green yarn.

ROW 18: 1 dec, 7 sc, 1 dec, ch 1 and turn (9 sc total)

ROW 19: 1 dec, 5 sc, 1 dec, ch 1 and turn (7 sc total)

ROW 20: 1 dec, 3 sc, 1 dec, ch 1 and turn (5 sc total)

Now you are going to sc around the entire piece, working 1 sc in each st and in each row end around (63 sc total).

Finish with 1 sl.

Cut yarn and fasten off all threads.

Attach a pair of 5-mm safety eyes between rows 16 and 17 with 5 st between them.

Embroider a black mouth using black embroidery floss in the middle of row 15. Have fun with the expression!

AVOCADO BACK

Using your Dark Green yarn, start with a magic ring.

RND 1: 5 sc into the magic ring (5 sc total)

RND 2: [1 inc] 5 times (10 sc total)

RND 3: [1 sc, 1 inc] 5 times (15 sc total)

RND 4: [2 sc, 1 inc] 5 times (20 sc total)

RND 5: [3 sc, 1 inc] 5 times (30 sc total)

RND 6: [4 sc, 1 inc] 5 times (35 sc total)

RND 7: [5 sc, 1 inc] 5 times (40 sc total)

RND 8: [6 sc, 1 inc] 5 times (45 sc total)

RND 9: [7 sc, 1 inc] 5 times (50 sc total)

RND 10: [8 sc, 1 inc] 5 times (55 sc total)

RND 11: [9 sc, 1 inc] 5 times (60 sc total)

ROW 12: 1 inc, 7 sc, 1 inc, ch 1 and turn leaving the remaining sts unworked (11 sc total)

Now work back and forth in rows for the rest of the piece.

ROW 13-15: 11 sc, ch 1 and turn (3 rows, [11 sc in each row])

ROW 16: 1 dec, 7 sc, 1 dec, ch 1 and turn (9 sc total)

ROW 17: 1 dec, 5 sc, 1 dec, ch 1 and turn (7 sc total)

ROW 18: 1 dec, 3 sc, 1 dec, ch 1 and turn (5 sc total)

Now you are going to sc around the whole piece, working 1 sc in each st and in each row end around (63 sc total).

Put the Front on top of the Back of the Avocado.

Sc the two pieces together, working 1 sc through both layers in each st to join, using your Dark Green yarn.

Don't forget to stuff the Avocado before you sc it all together.

CHEEKS (MAKE 2)

Using your Pink yarn, start with a magic ring.

RND 1: 6 sc into the magic ring (6 sc total)

Finish with 1 sl.

Cut yarn but leave a long tail for sewing. Pin the Cheeks to the Avocado and sew them on.

LEGS (MAKE 2)

Using your Brown yarn, ch 4.

RND 1: Starting in the second ch from the hook, 2 sc, 3 sc in the next ch, turn around the corner and work in the loops on the other side of the chain, 1 sc, 2 sc in the next ch (8 sc total).

RND 2: 1 inc, 1 sc, [1 inc] 3 times, 1 sc, 1 inc, 1 sc (13 sc total)

RND 3: 5 sc, 3 hdc, 5 sc (13 st total)

RND 4: 4 sc, 1 dec, 2 sc, 1 dec, 3 sc (11 sc total)

RND 5: [1 dec] 5 times, 1 sc (6 sc total)

Stuff the feet.

RND 6-10: 6 sc (5 rounds, [6 sc in each round])

Cut yarn but leave a long tail for sewing.

Pin the Legs to the Avocado and sew them on.

ARMS (MAKE 2)

Using your Brown yarn, start with a magic ring.

RND 1: 6 sc into the magic ring (6 sc total)

RND 2-6: 6 sc (5 rounds, [6 sc in each round])

Finish with 1 sl.

Cut yarn but leave a long tail for sewing. Pin the Arms to the Avocado and sew them on.

Girls Just Wanna Have Sun

CUTE, COZY PATTERNS NO MATTER THE WEATHER

After rain and clouds come sunshine and rainbows . . . and sunflowers! Yes, in this chapter you will find patterns to make an amigurumi doll for whatever the weather brings you! Make a Smiling Sunshine (page 66) to brighten up a rainy day, or crochet a Cute Cloud (page 57) when you need a bit of shade at the height of summer.

In this chapter, you will find four beginner-friendly patterns and one pattern that is a little bit more challenging: the Sensational Sunflower (page 69). It is one of the longer patterns in the book and requires a bit more sewing than the rest of the patterns, which makes it a great pattern to practice your assembling skills! Alternatively, if you are looking for a quick and easy pattern, the Cute Cloud (page 57) is a great choice. Not only does it require a small amount of yarn, but it is also super, duper cute! Make one for each color of the rainbow, because who says clouds need to be white? Of course, my favorite pattern in this chapter is the Good Luck Raindrop (page 63)—I carry one in my purse wherever I go for good luck!

Cute Cloud

Who doesn't love a Cute Cloud?! This cloud is a quick make and only requires a small amount of yarn. So it's a win-win! You will begin by crocheting the left side of the cloud and then you will use increases and decreases to make the fluffy bumps on the top of it. Finish it off with some cute legs, and you have a cloud fit for any blue sky!

SKILL LEVEL: BEGINNER

MATERIALS

Light fingering weight yarn in White, Pink and Blue

US B/1 (2.25-mm) hook

A pair of 6-mm safety eyes

Tapestry needle

Black embroidery floss

Polyester stuffing

ABBREVIATIONS

rnd: round

ch: chain

sc: single crochet

1 inc: single crochet 2 stitches into the same stitch

1 dec: single crochet 2 stitches together

hdc: half double crochet

sl: slip stitch

st(s): stitch(es)

Approximate size for a finished Cute Cloud: 4.3 x 2.3 inches (11 x 6 cm)

Cute Cloud Pattern

CLOUD

Using your White yarn, start with a magic ring.

RND 1: 6 sc into the magic ring (6 sc total)

RND 2: [1 inc] 6 times (12 sc total)

RND 3: [1 sc, 1 inc] 6 times (18 sc total)

RND 4: [2 sc, 1 inc] 6 times (24 sc total)

RND 5–8: 24 sc (4 rounds, [24 sc in each round])

RND 9: 10 sc, [1 dec] 2 times, 10 sc (22 sc total)

RND 10: 10 sc, [1 inc] 2 times, 10 sc (24 sc total)

RND 11: 11 sc, [1 inc] 3 times, 10 sc (27 sc total)

RND 12: 12 sc, [1 inc] 3 times, 12 sc (30 sc total)

RND 13: 14 sc, [1 inc] 3 times, 13 sc (33 sc total)

RND 14–21: 33 sc (8 rounds, [33 sc in each round])

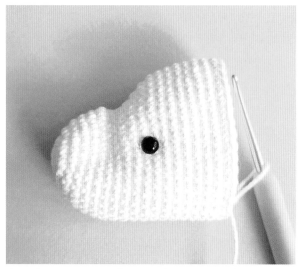

Attach one 6-mm safety eye between Rnds 13 and 14.

Attach the second eye between Rnds 21 and 22, placing it in line with the first eye.

Now it's time to attach the first safety eye. Attach one 6-mm safety eye between rounds 13 and 14.

RND 22: 15 sc, [1 dec] 3 times, 12 sc (30 sc total)

RND 23: 14 sc, [1 dec] 3 times, 10 sc (27 sc total)

RND 24: 12 sc, [1 dec] 3 times, 9 sc (24 sc total)

Now it's time to attach the second safety eye. Attach it between rounds 21 and 22. Make sure you place it in line with the first eye.

RND 25: 12 sc, [1 dec] 2 times, 8 sc (22 sc total)

RND 26: 12 sc [1 inc] 2 times, 8 sc (24 sc total)

Start stuffing, referring to the guide on page 11.

RND 27–30: 24 sc (4 rounds, [24 sc in each round])

RND 31: [2 sc, 1 dec] 6 times (18 sc total)

RND 32: [1 sc, 1 dec] 6 times (12 sc total)

RND 33: [1 dec] 6 times (6 sc total)

Cut yarn and fasten off all threads.

Embroider a black mouth using black embroidery floss.

CHEEKS (MAKE 2)

Using your Pink yarn, start with a magic ring.

RND 1: 6 sc into the magic ring (6 sc total)

Finish with 1 sl.

Cut yarn but leave a long tail for sewing. Pin the Cheeks to the Cloud and sew them on.

LEGS (MAKE 2)

Using your Blue yarn, ch 4.

RND 1: Starting in the second ch from the hook, 2 sc, 3 sc in the next ch, turn around the corner and working in the loops on the other side of the chain, 1 sc, 2 sc in the next ch (8 sc total).

RND 2: 1 inc, 1 sc, [1 inc] 3 times, 1 sc, 1 inc, 1 sc (13 sc total)

RND 3: 5 sc, 3 hdc, 5 sc (13 st total)

RND 4: 4 sc, 1 dec, 2 sc, 1 dec, 3 sc (11 sc total)

RND 5: [1 dec] 5 times, 1 sc (6 sc total)

Stuff the feet.

RND 6–9: 6 sc (4 rounds, [6 sc in each round])

Cut yarn but leave a long tail for sewing.

Pin the Legs to the Cloud and sew them on.

Rainbow Vibes

This bright rainbow is made in one round piece that you then fold and slip stitch together across the top. The arms and legs add a fun touch to it. Feel free to make one version with typical colors, but why not make a pastel rainbow, too? Unleash all your favorite colors and make a rainbow that's worth smiling about!

SKILL LEVEL: BEGINNER

MATERIALS

Light fingering weight yarn in Purple, Blue, Green, Yellow, Orange, Hot Pink, Pink and Light Blue

US B/1 (2.25-mm) hook

Tapestry needle

Black embroidery floss

A pair of 6-mm safety eyes

Polyester stuffing

ABBREVIATIONS

rnd: round

ch: chain

sc: single crochet

1 inc: single crochet 2 stitches into the same stitch

1 dec: single crochet 2 stitches together

hdc: half double crochet

sl: slip stitch

st(s): stitch(es)

Approximate size for a finished Rainbow Vibes: 4 x 2.5 inches (10 x 6 cm)

Rainbow Vibes Pattern

RAINBOW

Using your Purple yarn, ch 24, join with 1 sl to the first ch to make a ring.

RND 1: Working into each ch, [3 sc, 1 inc] 6 times (30 sc total)

RND 2: 2 sc, 1 inc [4 sc, 1 inc] 5 times, 2 sc (36 sc total)

Change to Blue.

RND 3: [5 sc, 1 inc] 6 times (42 sc total)

RND 4: 3 sc, 1 inc [6 sc, 1 inc] 5 times, 3 sc (48 sc total)

Change to Green.

RND 5: [7 sc, 1 inc] 6 times (54 sc total)

RND 6: 4 sc, 1 inc [8 sc, 1 inc] 5 times, 4 sc (60 sc total)

Change to Yellow.

RND 7: [9 sc, 1 inc] 6 times (66 sc total)

RND 8: 5 sc, 1 inc [10 sc, 1 inc] 5 times, 5 sc (72 sc total)

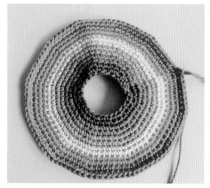

After Rnd 12, your piece should look like this.

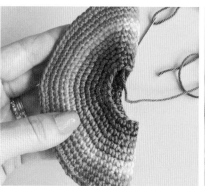

Fold your piece in half down the middle.

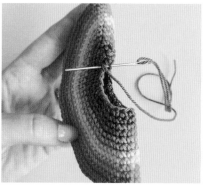

Sew the bottom purple part of the rainbow together using your Purple yarn.

After you have sewn the Purple part together, it should look like this.

Slip stitch the top Hot Pink part together.

Change to Orange.

RND 9: [11 sc, 1 inc] 6 times (78 sc total)

RND 10: 6 sc, 1 inc [12 sc, 1 inc] 5 times, 6 sc (84 sc total)

Change to Hot Pink.

RND 11: [13 sc, 1 inc] 6 times (90 sc total)

RND 12: 7 sc, 1 inc [14 sc, 1 inc] 5 times, 7 sc (96 sc total)

Do not cut your yarn.

Fold your piece in the middle.

Embroider a black mouth in the middle of round 4 using black embroidery floss.

Attach a pair of 6-mm safety eyes between rounds 5 and 4 with 6 st between them.

Sew the bottom Purple part of the rainbow together using your Purple yarn.

Slip stitch the top Hot Pink part together; don't forget to stuff it as you work.

CHEEKS (MAKE 2)

Using your Pink yarn, start with a magic ring.

RND 1: 6 sc into the magic ring (6 sc total)

Finish with 1 sl.

Cut your yarn but leave a long tail for sewing. Pin the Cheeks to the Rainbow and sew them on.

LEGS (MAKE 2)

Using your Light Blue yarn, ch 4.

RND 1: Starting in the second ch from the hook, 2 sc, 3 sc in the next ch, turn around the corner and working in the loops on the other side of the chain, 1 sc, 2 sc in the next ch (8 sc total).

RND 2: 1 inc, 1 sc, [1 inc] 3 times, 1 sc, 1 inc, 1 sc (13 sc total)

RND 3: 5 sc, 3 hdc, 5 sc (13 st total)

RND 4: 4 sc, 1 dec, 2 sc, 1 dec, 3 sc (11 sc total)

RND 5: [1 dec] 5 times, 1 sc (6 sc total)

Stuff the feet.

RND 6–9: 6 sc (4 rounds, [6 sc in each round])

Cut yarn but leave a long tail for sewing.

Pin the Legs to the Rainbow and sew them on.

ARMS (MAKE 2)

Using your Light Blue yarn, start with a magic ring.

RND 1: 6 sc into the magic ring (6 sc total)

RND 2–6: 6 sc (5 rounds, [6 sc in each round])

Finish with 1 sl.

Cut yarn but leave a long tail for sewing. Pin the Arms to the Rainbow and sew them on.

Good Luck Raindrop

They say rain on your wedding day means good luck, but I'm hoping this raindrop will bring you good luck every day! This chubby little raindrop is made starting at the bottom and working your way up. The arms and legs are then sewn onto it. It is a beginner-friendly pattern and is made pretty quickly—the perfect project for a rainy day!

SKILL LEVEL: BEGINNER

MATERIALS

Light fingering weight yarn in Blue, Pink and Light Blue
US B/1 (2.25-mm) hook
A pair of 5-mm safety eyes
Tapestry needle
Black embroidery floss
Polyester stuffing

ABBREVIATIONS

rnd: round
ch: chain
sc: single crochet
1 inc: single crochet 2 stitches into the same stitch
1 dec: single crochet 2 stitches together
hdc: half double crochet
sl: slip stitch
st(s): stitch(es)

Approximate size for a finished Good Luck Raindrop: 3 x 3 inches (8 x 8 cm)

Good Luck Raindrop Pattern

RAINDROP

Using your Blue yarn, start with a magic ring.

RND 1: 6 sc into the magic ring (6 sc total)

RND 2: [1 inc] 6 times (12 sc total)

RND 3: [1 sc, 1 inc] 6 times (18 sc total)

RND 4: 1 sc, 1 inc [2 sc, 1 inc] 5 times, 1 sc (24 sc total)

RND 5: [3 sc, 1 inc] 6 times (30 sc total)

RND 6: 2 sc, 1 inc [4 sc, 1 inc] 5 times, 2 sc (36 sc total)

RND 7: [5 sc, 1 inc] 6 times (42 sc total)

RND 8: 3 sc, 1 inc [6 sc, 1 inc] 5 times, 2 sc (48 sc total)

RND 9–15: 48 sc (7 rounds, [48 sc in each round])

RND 16: 3 sc, 1 dec [6 sc, 1 dec] 5 times, 3 sc (42 sc total)

RND 17: 42 sc (42 sc total)

RND 18: [5 sc, 1 dec] 6 times (36 sc total)

RND 19: 36 sc (36 sc total)

RND 20: 2 sc, 1 dec [4 sc, 1 dec] 5 times, 2 sc (30 sc total)

RND 21: 30 sc (30 sc total)

Now it's time to attach the 5-mm safety eyes. Attach them between rounds 16 and 17 with 5 st between.

Embroider a black mouth in the middle of round 15 using black embroidery floss.

RND 22: [3 sc, 1 dec] 6 times (24 sc total)

RND 23: 24 sc (24 sc total)

Start stuffing, referring to the guide on page 11.

RND 24: 1 sc, 1 dec [2 sc, 1 dec] 5 times, 1 sc (18 sc total)

RND 25: 18 sc (18 sc total)

RND 26: [1 sc, 1 dec] 6 times (12 sc total)

RND 27: 12 sc (12 sc total)

RND 28: [1 dec] 6 times (6 sc total)

Cut yarn and fasten off all threads.

CHEEKS (MAKE 2)

Using your Pink yarn, start with a magic ring.

RND 1: 6 sc into the magic ring (6 sc total)

Finish with 1 sl.

Cut yarn but leave a long tail for sewing. Pin the Cheeks to the Raindrop and sew them on.

LEGS (MAKE 2)

Using your Light Blue yarn, ch 4.

RND 1: Starting in the second ch from the hook, 2 sc, 3 sc in the next ch, turn around the corner and working in the loops on the other side of the chain, 1 sc, 2 sc in the next ch (8 sc total).

RND 2: 1 inc, 1 sc, [1 inc] 3 times, 1 sc, 1 inc, 1 sc (13 sc total)

RND 3: 5 sc, 3 hdc, 5 sc (13 st total)

RND 4: 4 sc, 1 dec, 2 sc, 1 dec, 3 sc (11 sc total)

RND 5: [1 dec] 5 times, 1 sc (6 sc total)

Stuff the feet.

RND 6–9: 6 sc (4 rounds, [6 sc in each round])

Cut yarn but leave a long tail for sewing.

Pin the Legs to the Raindrop and sew them on.

ARMS (MAKE 2)

Using your Light Blue yarn, start with a magic ring.

RND 1: 6 sc into the magic ring (6 sc total)

RND 2–6: 6 sc (5 rounds, [6 sc in each round])

Finish with 1 sl.

Cut yarn but leave a long tail for sewing. Pin the Arms to the Raindrop and sew them on.

Smiling Sunshine

Needing some sunshine in your life? Then this is the pattern for you! The sun is made starting with the yellow middle piece, then adding the sunbeams one by one. The legs are added to it last as a fun, final touch for a smiling sun that can go wherever you'd like it to!

SKILL LEVEL: BEGINNER

MATERIALS

Light fingering weight yarn in Yellow, Orange, Pink and Light Blue

US B/1 (2.25-mm) hook

A pair of 5-mm safety eyes

Tapestry needle

Black embroidery floss

Polyester stuffing

ABBREVIATIONS

rnd: round

ch: chain

sc: single crochet

1 inc: single crochet 2 stitches into the same stitch

1 dec: single crochet 2 stitches together

hdc: half double crochet

sl: slip stitch

st(s): stitch(es)

Approximate size for a finished Smiling Sunshine: 4 x 4.3 inches (10 x 11 cm)

Smiling Sunshine Pattern

SUN

Using your Yellow yarn, start with a magic ring.

RND 1: 6 sc into the magic ring (6 sc total)

RND 2: [1 inc] 6 times (12 sc total)

RND 3: [1 sc, 1 inc] 6 times (18 sc total)

RND 4: 1 sc, 1 inc [2 sc, 1 inc] 5 times, 1 sc (24 sc total)

RND 5: [3 sc, 1 inc] 6 times (30 sc total)

RND 6: 2 sc, 1 inc [4 sc, 1 inc] 5 times, 2 sc (36 sc total)

RND 7: [5 sc, 1 inc] 6 times (42 sc total)

RND 8: 3 sc, 1 inc [6 sc, 1 inc] 5 times, 3 sc (48 sc total)

RND 9–11: 48 sc (3 rounds, [48 sc in each round])

RND 12: 3 sc, 1 dec [6 sc, 1 dec] 5 times, 3 sc (42 sc total)

RND 13: [5 sc, 1 dec] 6 times (36 sc total)

Now it's time to attach the safety eyes. Attach a pair of 5-mm safety eyes between rounds 4 and 5 approximately 6 st apart. Embroider a black mouth in the middle of the Sun using black embroidery floss.

Before sewing on the sunbeams, your piece should look like this.

SUNBEAMS (MAKE 8)

Using your Orange yarn, start with a magic ring.

RND 1: 6 sc into the magic ring (6 sc total)

RND 2: 6 sc (6 sc total)

RND 3: [1 inc] 6 times (12 sc total)

RND 4–7: 12 sc (4 rounds, [12 sc in each round])

Cut yarn but leave a long tail for sewing.

Pin the Sunbeams to the Sun and sew them on one by one.

CHEEKS (MAKE 2)

Using your Pink yarn, start with a magic ring.

RND 1: 6 sc into the magic ring (6 sc total)

Finish with 1 sl.

Cut your yarn but leave a long tail for sewing. Pin the Cheeks to the Sunshine and sew them on.

LEGS (MAKE 2)

Using your Light Blue yarn, ch 4.

RND 1: Starting in the second ch from the hook, 2 sc, 3 sc in the same ch, turn around the corner and working in the loops on the other side of the chain, 1 sc, 2 sc in the same ch (8 sc total).

RND 2: 1 inc, 1 sc, [1 inc] 3 times, 1 sc, 1 inc, 1 sc (13 sc total)

RND 3: 5 sc, 3 hdc, 5 sc (13 st total)

RND 4: 4 sc, 1 dec, 2 sc, 1 dec, 3 sc (11 sc total)

RND 5: [1 dec] 5 times, 1 sc (6 sc total)

Stuff the feet.

RND 6–9: 6 sc (4 rounds, [6 sc in each round])

Fasten off and leave a long yarn tail for sewing.

Pin the Legs to the Sunshine and sew them on.

Sensational Sunflower

Sun and flowers always make me happy, so why not combine them into a Sensational Sunflower? In this project, you will start by making the sunflower bud, then you will crochet and sew the petals onto it. The pot is also made separately, then it is finished by adding a stalk onto which you will sew your sunflower!

SKILL LEVEL: INTERMEDIATE

MATERIALS

Light fingering weight yarn in Orange, Pink, Yellow, Lilac, Light Blue, Green, Light Yellow, Light Orange and Brown

US B/1 (2.25-mm) hook

Tapestry needle

Black embroidery floss

A pair of 4-mm safety eyes

Polyester stuffing

A small piece of cardboard

Sewing thread

ABBREVIATIONS

rnd: round

ch: chain

sc: single crochet

1 inc: single crochet 2 stitches into the same stitch

1 dec: single crochet 2 stitches together

sl: slip stitch

st(s): stitch(es)

Approximate size for a finished Sensational Sunflower: 6 x 3.5 inches (15 x 9 cm)

Sensational Sunflower Pattern

SUNFLOWER BUD

Using your Orange yarn, start with a magic ring.

RND 1: 6 sc into the magic ring (6 sc total)

RND 2: [1 inc] 6 times (12 sc total)

RND 3: [1 sc, 1 inc] 6 times (18 sc total)

RND 4: 1 sc, 1 inc [2 sc, 1 inc] 5 times, 1 sc (24 sc total)

RND 5: [3 sc, 1 inc] 6 times (30 sc total)

RND 6: 2 sc, 1 inc [4 sc, 1 inc] 5 times, 2 sc (36 sc total)

RND 7–9: 36 sc (3 rounds, [36 sc in each round])

RND 10: 2 sc, 1 dec [4 sc, 1 dec] 5 times, 2 sc (30 sc total)

Now it's time to attach the safety eyes and embroider a mouth and cheeks.

Embroider a mouth between rounds 1 and 2 using black embroidery floss.

Attach a pair of 4-mm safety eyes between rounds 3 and 4, making sure they are in line with each other.

Embroider cheeks using Pink yarn.

RND 11: [3 sc, 1 dec] 6 times (24 sc total)

RND 12: 1 sc, 1 dec [2 sc, 1 dec] 5 times, 1 sc (18 sc total)

Start stuffing, referring to the guide on page 11.

RND 13: [1 sc, 1 dec] 6 times (12 sc total)

RND 14: [1 dec] 6 times (6 sc total)

Cut yarn and fasten off all threads.

PETALS (MAKE 5)

Using your Yellow yarn, start with a magic ring.

RND 1: 6 sc into the magic ring (6 sc total)

RND 2: [1 inc] 6 times (12 sc total)

RND 3: [1 sc, 1 inc] 6 times (18 sc total)

RND 4–8: 18 sc (5 rounds, [18 sc in each round])

RND 9: [1 sc, 1 dec] 6 times (12 sc total)

Finish with 1 sl.

Cut yarn but leave a long tail for sewing.

Press the Petals flat with your hands, if necessary.

Pin them to the Sunflower Bud and sew them on one by one.

POT

Using your Lilac yarn, start with a magic ring.

RND 1: 6 sc into the magic ring (6 sc total)

RND 2: [1 inc] 6 times (12 sc total)

RND 3: [1 sc, 1 inc] 6 times (18 sc total)

RND 4: 1 sc, 1 inc [2 sc, 1 inc] 5 times, 1 sc (24 sc total)

RND 5: [3 sc, 1 inc] 6 times (30 sc total)

RND 6: In back loops only, 30 sc (30 sc total)

RND 7: 30 sc (30 sc total)

Change to Light Blue.

RND 8: 30 sc (30 sc total)

RND 9: 2 sc, 1 inc [4 sc, 1 inc] 5 times, 2 sc (36 sc total)

Change to Green.

RND 10–11: 36 sc (2 rounds, [36 sc in each round])

Change to Light Yellow.

RND 12: 36 sc (36 sc total)

RND 13: [5 sc, 1 inc] 6 times (42 sc total)

Change to Light Orange.

RND 14–15: 42 sc (2 rounds, [42 sc in each round])

Change to Pink.

RND 16: In front loops only, 42 sc (42 sc total)

RND 17: 42 sc (42 sc total)

Finish with 1 sl.

Cut yarn and fasten off all threads.

Put your work onto a piece of cardboard and cut out a piece that's the same size as the bottom of the Pot. Place the cardboard piece inside the bottom of the Pot to give it more stability. Do not start stuffing the Pot just yet.

SOIL

Using your Brown yarn, rejoin in one of the back loops of round 16 on the Pot.

RND 1: In remaining back loops of round 16, [5 sc, 1 dec] 6 times (36 sc total)

RND 2: 2 sc, 1 dec [4 sc, 1 dec] 5 times, 2 sc (30 sc total)

RND 3: [3 sc, 1 dec] 6 times (24 sc total)

Now you should start stuffing your Pot, referring to the guide on page 11.

RND 4: 1 sc, 1 dec [2 sc, 1 dec] 5 times, 1 sc (18 sc total)

RND 5: [1 sc, 1 dec] 6 times (12 sc total)

RND 6: [1 dec] 6 times (6 sc total)

Cut yarn and fasten off all threads.

STALK

Using your Green yarn, start with a magic ring.

RND 1: 5 sc into the magic ring (5 sc total)

RND 2: [1 inc] 5 times (10 sc total)

Start stuffing once you have made a few rounds, and keep stuffing a little at a time as you crochet more rounds.

RND 3–7: 10 sc (5 rounds, [10 sc in each round])

Cut yarn but leave a long tail for sewing.

Pin the Stalk to the Soil and sew it on.

Pin your Sunflower on top of the Stalk and sew it on using sewing thread.

It's Food O'Clock

MEALS MADE WITH LOVE

You can't just have sweets all the time, right? You need to add some heartier foods into your diet as well. In this case, we're talking mostly fast food, because it is delicious, super cute and works up nice and quickly! Start with a hamburger and fries, then add a slice of pizza and finish it off with some pancakes and lemonade. When you're all done, this fast-food feast is sure to be a treat for the eyes—enjoy!

Many of the projects in this chapter are also the perfect play food to gift to a child, because who says you can't play with your food? And speaking of playing with foods, the Fri-Day Fries (page 95) are perfect for that. You can make them with a small amount of yarn in no time at all! You can also make a Cheesy Burger (page 90) with some fresh lettuce, bright tomatoes, a juicy patty and, of course, the cheese. Stack it up and you have yourself a tasty burger, or play around with the colors and toppings to make it totally vegetarian—it's up to you!

With all that said, my favorite pattern in this chapter has to be the Sour & Sweet Lemonade (page 87). This pattern has so many possibilities—use a different color palette and turn it into a whole new drink!

Piece of Pizza Cuteness

The pizza is made in separate pieces that you will join together with single crochet. The topping is then sewn onto it. This Piece of Pizza Cuteness is a pepperoni pizza, but you can of course skip the meat and make them into red tomatoes if you're a vegetarian!

SKILL LEVEL: BEGINNER

MATERIALS

Light fingering weight yarn in Red, Beige, Pink, Yellow and Burgundy
US B/1 (2.25-mm) hook
Tapestry needle
Black embroidery floss
A pair of 4-mm safety eyes
Polyester stuffing

ABBREVIATIONS

rnd: round
ch: chain
sc: single crochet
1 inc: single crochet 2 stitches into the same stitch
1 dec: single crochet 2 stitches together
hdc: half double crochet
sl: slip stitch
st(s): stitch(es)

Approximate size for a finished Piece of Pizza Cuteness: 4.3 x 3.5 inches (11 x 9 cm)

Piece of Pizza Cuteness Pattern

PIZZA FRONT

Using your Red yarn, ch 2.

ROW 1: Starting in the second ch from the hook, 1 inc, ch 1 (does not count as st throughout), and turn (2 sc total).

ROW 2: [1 inc] 2 times, ch 1 and turn (4 sc total)

ROW 3: 4 sc, ch 1 and turn (4 sc total)

ROW 4: 1 inc, 2 sc, 1 inc, ch 1 and turn (6 sc total)

ROW 5: 6 sc, ch 1 and turn (6 sc total)

ROW 6: 1 inc, 4 sc, 1 inc, ch 1 and turn (8 sc total)

ROW 7: 8 sc, ch 1 and turn (8 sc total)

ROW 8: 1 inc, 6 sc, 1 inc, ch 1 and turn (10 sc total)

ROW 9: 10 sc, ch 1 and turn (10 sc total)

ROW 10: 1 inc, 8 sc, 1 inc, ch 1 and turn (12 sc total)

ROW 11: 12 sc, ch 1 and turn (12 sc total)

ROW 12: 1 inc, 10 sc, 1 inc, ch 1 and turn (14 sc total)

ROW 13: 14 sc, ch 1 and turn (14 sc total)

ROW 14: 1 inc, 12 sc, 1 inc, ch 1 and turn (16 sc total)

ROW 15–16: 16 sc, ch 1 and turn (2 rows [16 sc in each row])

ROW 17: 1 inc, 14 sc, 1 inc, ch 1 and turn (18 sc total)

ROW 18–19: 18 sc, ch 1 and turn (2 rows [18 sc in each row])

ROW 20: 1 inc, 16 sc, 1 inc, ch 1 and turn (20 sc total)

ROW 21–22: 20 sc, ch 1 and turn (2 rows [20 sc in each row])

ROW 23: 1 inc, 18 sc, 1 inc, ch 1 and turn (22 sc total)

ROW 24–25: 22 sc, ch 1 and turn (2 rows [22 sc in each row])

ROW 26: 1 inc, 20 sc, 1 inc, ch 1 and turn (24 sc total)

Change to Beige.

ROW 27: In back loops only, 24 sc, ch 1 and turn (24 sc total)

ROW 28–31: 24 sc, ch 1 and turn (4 rounds [24 sc in each row])

Cut yarn and fasten off all threads.

Embroider a mouth between rounds 28 and 29.

Attach a pair of 4-mm safety eyes between rounds 29 and 30 with 5 st between them.

PIZZA BACK

Using your Beige yarn, ch 2.

ROW 1: Starting in the second ch from the hook, 1 inc, ch 1 (does not count as st throughout), and turn (2 sc total).

ROW 2: [1 inc] 2 times, ch 1 and turn (4 sc total)

ROW 3: 4 sc, ch 1 and turn (4 sc total)

ROW 4: 1 inc, 2 sc, 1 inc, ch 1 and turn (6 sc total)

ROW 5: 6 sc, ch 1 and turn (6 sc total)

ROW 6: 1 inc, 4 sc, 1 inc, ch 1 and turn (8 sc total)

ROW 7: 8 sc, ch 1 and turn (8 sc total)

ROW 8: 1 inc, 6 sc, 1 inc, ch 1 and turn (10 sc total)

ROW 9: 10 sc, ch 1 and turn (10 sc total)

ROW 10: 1 inc, 8 sc, 1 inc, ch 1 and turn (12 sc total)

ROW 11: 12 sc, ch 1 and turn (12 sc total)

ROW 12: 1 inc, 10 sc, 1 inc, ch 1 and turn (14 sc total)

ROW 13: 14 sc, ch 1 and turn (14 sc total)

ROW 14: 1 inc, 12 sc, 1 inc, ch 1 and turn (16 sc total)

ROW 15–16: 16 sc, ch 1 and turn (2 rows [16 sc in each row])

ROW 17: 1 inc, 14 sc, 1 inc, ch 1 and turn (18 sc total)

ROW 18–19: 18 sc, ch 1 and turn (2 rows [18 sc in each row])

ROW 20: 1 inc, 16 sc, 1 inc, ch 1 and turn (20 sc total)

ROW 21–22: 20 sc, ch 1 and turn (2 rows [20 sc in each row])

ROW 23: 1 inc, 18 sc, 1 inc, ch 1 and turn (22 sc total)

ROW 24–25: 22 sc, ch 1 and turn (2 rows [22 sc in each row])

ROW 26: 1 inc, 20 sc, 1 inc, ch 1 and turn (24 sc total)

ROW 27–31: 24 sc, ch 1 and turn (5 rows [24 sc in each row])

Place the Pizza Front on top of the Pizza Back. Sc around the pizza with your Beige yarn, working through both layers to join, working 2 sc in each corner and leaving a gap for stuffing at the end.

Stuff lightly before you complete the sc seam.

Cut yarn and fasten off all threads.

CHEEKS (MAKE 2)

Using your Pink yarn, start with a magic ring.

RND 1: 6 sc into the magic ring (6 sc total)

Finish with 1 sl.

Cut yarn but leave a long tail for sewing. Pin the Cheeks to the Pizza and sew them on.

CHEESE

Using your Yellow yarn, ch 2.

ROW 1: Starting in the second ch from the hook, 1 inc, ch 1 (does not count as st throughout), and turn (2 sc total).

ROW 2: [1 inc] 2 times, ch 1 and turn (4 sc total)

ROW 3: 4 sc, ch 1 and turn (4 sc total)

ROW 4: 1 inc, 2 sc, 1 inc, ch 1 and turn (6 sc total)

ROW 5: 6 sc, ch 1 and turn (6 sc total)

ROW 6: 1 inc, 4 sc, 1 inc, ch 1 and turn (8 sc total)

ROW 7: 8 sc, ch 1 and turn (8 sc total)

ROW 8: 1 inc, 6 sc, 1 inc, ch 1 and turn (10 sc total)

ROW 9: 10 sc, ch 1 and turn (10 sc total)

ROW 10: 1 inc, 8 sc, 1 inc, ch 1 and turn (12 sc total)

ROW 11: 12 sc, ch 1 and turn (12 sc total)

ROW 12: 1 inc, 10 sc, 1 inc, ch 1 and turn (14 sc total)

ROW 13: 14 sc, ch 1 and turn (14 sc total)

ROW 14: 1 inc, 12 sc, 1 inc, ch 1 and turn (16 sc total)

ROW 15–16: 16 sc, ch 1 and turn (2 rows [16 sc in each row])

ROW 17: 1 inc, 14 sc, 1 inc, ch 1 and turn (18 sc total)

ROW 18–19: 18 sc, ch 1 and turn (2 rows [18 sc in each row])

ROW 20: 1 inc, 16 sc, 1 inc, ch 1 and turn (20 sc total)

ROW 21: 1 sc, *skip 1 st, 3 hdc in next st, skip 1 st, 2 sc in next st, skip 1 st, 3 hdc in next st*

Repeat from * to * to last st.

Finish with 1 sc in the last st.

Cut yarn but leave a long tail for sewing. Pin the Cheese to the Pizza and sew it on.

PEPPERONI (MAKE 3)

Using your Burgundy yarn, start with a magic ring.

RND 1: 6 sc into the magic ring (6 sc total)

RND 2: [1 inc] 6 times (12 sc total)

RND 3: [1 sc, 1 inc] 6 times (18 sc total)

Finish with 1 sl.

Cut yarn but leave a long tail for sewing. Pin the Pepperoni to the Pizza and sew it on.

Pretty Pancakes

Pancakes with whipped cream and strawberries? Yes, please! Each Pancake in this project is made separately and stacked together. You'll then sew the toppings onto the top of the stack—in this case, I've chosen whipped cream and strawberries for extra yumminess, but make sure you have fun with it, too! Why not bring in some of the toppings from other patterns in this book and really make these pancakes your own?

SKILL LEVEL: BEGINNER

MATERIALS

Light fingering weight yarn in Sand, Beige, Pink, White, Red and Green

US B/1 (2.25-mm) hook

Tapestry needle

Black embroidery floss

A pair of 4-mm safety eyes

Polyester stuffing

ABBREVIATIONS

rnd: round

ch: chain

sc: single crochet

1 inc: single crochet 2 stitches into the same stitch

1 dec: single crochet 2 stitches together

hdc: half double crochet

sl: slip stitch

st(s): stitch(es)

Approximate size for a finished Pretty Pancakes: 3 x 2.7 inches (8 x 7 cm)

Pretty Pancakes Pattern

TOP PANCAKE

Using your Sand yarn, start with a magic ring.

RND 1: 6 sc into the ring (6 sc total)

RND 2: [1 inc] 6 times (12 sc total)

RND 3: [1 sc, 1 inc] 6 times (18 sc total)

RND 4: 1 sc, 1 inc [2 sc, 1 inc] 5 times, 1 sc (24 sc total)

RND 5: [3 sc, 1 inc] 6 times (30 sc total)

RND 6: 2 sc, 1 inc [4 sc, 1 inc] 5 times, 2 sc (36 sc total)

RND 7: [5 sc, 1 inc] 6 times (42 sc total)

RND 8: 3 sc, 1 inc [6 sc, 1 inc] 5 times, 3 sc (48 sc total)

RND 9: [7 sc, 1 inc] 6 times (54 sc total)

RND 10: 4 sc, 1 inc [8 sc, 1 inc] 5 times, 4 sc (60 sc total)

RND 11: [9 sc, 1 inc] 6 times (66 sc total)

Change to Beige.

RND 12: In back loops only, 66 sc (66 sc total)

RND 13: [9 sc, 1 dec] 6 times (60 sc total)

RND 14: 4 sc, 1 dec [8 sc, 1 dec] 5 times, 4 sc (54 sc total)

RND 15: [7 sc, 1 dec] 6 times (48 sc total)

Now it's time to embroider the mouth and attach the eyes. Embroider a mouth between rounds 9 and 10 using black embroidery floss.

Attach a pair of 4-mm safety eyes between rounds 8 and 9 with 5 st in between them.

RND 16: 3 sc, 1 dec [6 sc, 1 dec] 5 times, 3 sc (42 sc total)

RND 17: [5 sc, 1 dec] 6 times (36 sc total)

RND 18: 2 sc, 1 dec [4 sc, 1 dec] 5 times, 2 sc (30 sc total)

RND 19: [3 sc, 1 dec] 6 times (24 sc total)

Start stuffing lightly, referring to the guide on page 11.

RND 20: 1 sc, 1 dec [2 sc, 1 dec] 5 times, 1 sc (18 sc total)

RND 21: [1 sc, 1 dec] 6 times (12 sc total)

RND 22: [1 dec] 6 times (6 sc total)

Cut yarn and fasten off all threads.

PANCAKES (MAKE 2)

Using your Sand yarn, start with a magic ring.

RND 1: 6 sc into the ring (6 sc total)

RND 2: [1 inc] 6 times (12 sc total)

RND 3: [1 sc, 1 inc] 6 times (18 sc total)

RND 4: 1 sc, 1 inc [2 sc, 1 inc] 5 times, 1 sc (24 sc total)

RND 5: [3 sc, 1 inc] 6 times (30 sc total)

RND 6: 2 sc, 1 inc [4 sc, 1 inc] 5 times, 2 sc (36 sc total)

RND 7: [5 sc, 1 inc] 6 times (42 sc total)

RND 8: 3 sc, 1 inc [6 sc, 1 inc] 5 times, 3 sc (48 sc total)

RND 9: [7 sc, 1 inc] 6 times (54 sc total)

RND 10: 4 sc, 1 inc [8 sc, 1 inc] 5 times, 4 sc (60 sc total)

RND 11: [9 sc, 1 inc] 6 times (66 sc total)

Change to Beige.

RND 12: In back loops only, 66 sc (66 sc total)

RND 13: [9 sc, 1 dec] 6 times (60 sc total)

RND 14: 4 sc, 1 dec [8 sc, 1 dec] 5 times, 4 sc (54 sc total)

RND 15: [7 sc, 1 dec] 6 times (48 sc total)

RND 16: 3 sc, 1 dec [6 sc, 1 dec] 5 times, 3 sc (42 sc total)

RND 17: [5 sc, 1 dec] 6 times (36 sc total)

RND 18: 2 sc, 1 dec [4 sc, 1 dec] 5 times, 2 sc (30 sc total)

RND 19: [3 sc, 1 dec] 6 times (24 sc total)

Start stuffing lightly, referring to the guide on page 11.

RND 20: 1 sc, 1 dec [2 sc, 1 dec] 5 times, 1 sc (18 sc total)

RND 21: [1 sc, 1 dec] 6 times (12 sc total)

RND 22: [1 dec] 6 times (6 sc total)

Cut yarn and fasten off all threads.

CHEEKS (MAKE 2)

Using your Pink yarn, start with a magic ring.

RND 1: 6 sc into the magic ring (6 sc total)

Finish with 1 sl.

Cut yarn but leave a long tail for sewing. Pin the Cheeks to the Top Pancake and sew them on.

WHIPPED CREAM

Using your White yarn, start with a magic ring.

RND 1: 6 sc into the magic ring (6 sc total)

RND 2: In back loops only, [1 inc] 6 times (12 sc total)

RND 3: In back loops only, [1 sc, 1 inc] 6 times (18 sc total)

RND 4: In back loops only, [2 sc, 1 inc] 6 times (24 sc total)

RND 5: In back loops only, [3 sc, 1 inc] 6 times (30 sc total)

Ch 1 (does not count as st), turn your work around and work 1 hdc in each remaining loop of round 5 (30 hdc total).

Continue with 1 hdc in each of the remaining loops all the way up to the top of the Whipped Cream.

Cut yarn but leave a long tail for sewing. Pin the Whipped Cream to the Top Pancake and sew it on.

STRAWBERRIES (MAKE 2)

Using your Red yarn, start with a magic ring.

RND 1: 6 sc into the magic ring (6 sc total)

RND 2: 6 sc (6 sc total)

RND 3: [1 inc] 6 times (12 sc total)

RND 4–5: 12 sc (2 rounds, [12 sc in each round])

Start stuffing your Strawberry.

RND 6: In back loops only, [1 dec] 6 times (6 sc total)

Sew the hole together and fasten off.

STRAWBERRY LEAVES (MAKE 2)

Using your Green yarn, start with a magic ring, but don't pull it together.

Ch 3, 1 sc in the second ch from the hook, 1 sc, 1 sl into the ring

Repeat from * to * 4 more times to create five Leaves.

Pull the magic ring closed.

Cut your yarn but leave a long tail for sewing. Sew the Leaves onto the Strawberry.

Pin the Strawberry on top of your Pretty Pancake and sew it on.

Sour & Sweet Lemonade

When life gives you lemons, crochet a lemonade, right? This Sour & Sweet Lemonade has one main piece, the glass, and then the rest is sewn on. Not a fan of lemonade? It's easy to make many different types of fruity drinks, just change up the colors. Maybe you prefer orange or grape juice?

SKILL LEVEL: INTERMEDIATE

MATERIALS

Light fingering weight yarn in Light Yellow, White, Pink, Yellow and Hot Pink
US B/1 (2.25-mm) hook
A small piece of cardboard
Tapestry needle
Black embroidery floss
A pair of 6-mm safety eyes
Polyester stuffing
White sewing thread

ABBREVIATIONS

rnd: round
ch: chain
sc: single crochet
1 inc: single crochet 2 stitches into the same stitch
1 dec: single crochet 2 stitches together
sl: slip stitch
st(s): stitch(es)

Approximate size for a finished Sour & Sweet Lemonade: 4.7 x 3.5 inches (12 x 9 cm)

Sour & Sweet Lemonade Pattern

GLASS

Using your Light Yellow yarn, start with a magic ring.

RND 1: 6 sc into the ring (6 sc total)

RND 2: [1 inc] 6 times (12 sc total)

RND 3: [1 sc, 1 inc] 6 times (18 sc total)

RND 4: 1 sc, 1 inc [2 sc, 1 inc] 5 times, 1 sc (24 sc total)

RND 5: [3 sc, 1 inc] 6 times (30 sc total)

RND 6: 2 sc, 1 inc [4 sc, 1 inc] 5 times, 2 sc (36 sc total)

RND 7: [5 sc, 1 inc] 6 times (42 sc total)

RND 8: 3 sc, 1 inc [6 sc, 1 inc] 5 times, 3 sc (48 sc total)

RND 9: In back loops only, 48 sc (48 sc total)

RND 10–28: 48 sc (19 rounds [48 sc in each round])

Change to White; do not cut Light Yellow.

RND 29: In front loops only, 48 sc (48 sc total)

RND 30–31: 48 sc (2 rounds [48 sc in each round])

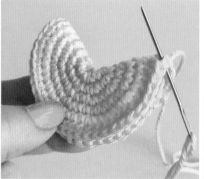
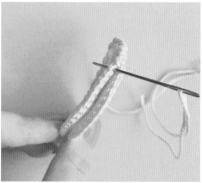

After Rnd 7, your lemon slice should look like this.

Fold the piece in half and insert your needle at one corner.

Sew the lemon slice together.

Cut your White yarn and fasten off.

Put your work on a piece of cardboard and cut out a piece that's the same size as the bottom. Place the cardboard piece in the bottom of the Glass. This will give more stability to your Glass.

Embroider a mouth in the middle of round 21 using black embroidery floss.

Attach a pair of 6-mm safety eyes between rounds 22 and 23 with 6 st in between them.

Pick up your Light Yellow yarn.

RND 1: In remaining back loops of round 29, 3 sc, 1 dec [6 sc, 1 dec] 5 times, 3 sc (42 sc total)

RND 2: [5 sc, 1 dec] 6 times (36 sc total)

RND 3: 2 sc, 1 dec [4 sc, 1 dec] 5 times, 2 sc (30 sc total)

Start stuffing, referring to the guide on page 11.

RND 4: [3 sc, 1 dec] 6 times (24 sc total)

RND 5: 1 sc, 1 dec [2 sc, 1 dec] 5 times, 1 sc (18 sc total)

RND 6: [1 sc, 1 dec] 6 times (12 sc total)

RND 7: [1 dec] 6 times (6 sc total)

Cut yarn and fasten off all threads.

CHEEKS (MAKE 2)

Using your Pink yarn, start with a magic ring.

RND 1: 6 sc into the magic ring (6 sc total)

Finish with 1 sl.

Cut yarn but leave a long tail for sewing. Pin the Cheeks to the Glass and sew them on.

HANDLE

Using your White yarn, start with a magic ring.

RND 1: 6 sc into the ring (6 sc total)

RND 2–16: 6 sc (15 rounds [6 sc in each round])

Cut yarn but leave a long tail for sewing.

Pin the Handle to the side of the Glass and sew it on.

LEMON SLICE

Using your Light Yellow yarn, start with a magic ring.

RND 1: 10 sc into the ring (10 sc total)

RND 2: [1 inc] 10 times (20 sc total)

RND 3: [1 sc, 1 inc] 10 times (30 sc total)

RND 4: 1 sc, 1 inc, [2 sc, 1 inc] 9 times, 1 sc (40 sc total)

RND 5: [3 sc, 1 inc] 10 times (50 sc total)

Change to White.

RND 6: 2 sc, 1 inc [4 sc, 1 inc] 9 times, 2 sc (60 sc total)

Change to Yellow.

RND 7: 60 sc (60 sc total)

Cut yarn but leave a long tail for sewing. Fasten off the other threads.

Fold the piece and sew it together.

Embroider wedges using your White yarn.

Pin the Lemon Slice to your Glass and sew it on using your White sewing thread.

STRAW

Using your Hot Pink yarn, start with a magic ring.

RND 1: 6 sc into the ring (6 sc total)

RND 2: In back loops only, 6 sc (6 sc total)

Change to White.

RND 3–4: 6 sc (2 rounds [6 sc in each round])

Change to Hot Pink.

RND 5: 1 dec, 2 sc, 1 inc, 1 sc (6 sc total)

RND 6: 1 dec, 2 sc, 1 inc, 1 sc (6 sc total)

Change to White.

RND 7–8: 6 sc (2 rounds [6 sc in each round])

Change to Hot Pink.

RND 9–10: 6 sc (2 rounds [6 sc in each round])

Change to White.

RND 11–12: 6 sc (2 rounds [6 sc in each round])

Cut yarn but leave a long tail for sewing.

Pin the Straw on top of your Glass of lemonade and sew it on.

Cheesy Burger

The Cheesy Burger is made in separate pieces. First you make the buns, then you make the tasty things to go inside the burger! This is the perfect gift for a hamburger-loving friend because they can stack up their own hamburger in any way they'd like!

SKILL LEVEL: INTERMEDIATE

MATERIALS

Light fingering weight yarn in Sand, Beige, Pink, Brown, Green, Yellow and Red
US B/1 (2.25-mm) hook
Tapestry needle
Black embroidery floss
A pair of 4-mm safety eyes
Polyester stuffing

ABBREVIATIONS

rnd: round
ch: chain
sc: single crochet
1 inc: single crochet 2 stitches into the same stitch
1 dec: single crochet 2 stitches together
dc: double crochet
sl: slip stitch
st(s): stitch(es)

Approximate size for a finished Cheesy Burger: 3.5 x 2.7 inches (9 x 7 cm)

Cheesy Burger Pattern

TOP BUN

Using your Sand yarn, start with a magic ring.

RND 1: 6 sc into the ring (6 sc total)

RND 2: [1 inc] 6 times (12 sc total)

RND 3: [1 sc, 1 inc] 6 times (18 sc total)

RND 4: 1 sc, 1 inc [2 sc, 1 inc] 5 times, 1 sc (24 sc total)

RND 5: [3 sc, 1 inc] 6 times (30 sc total)

RND 6: 2 sc, 1 inc [4 sc, 1 inc] 5 times, 2 sc (36 sc total)

RND 7: [5 sc, 1 inc] 6 times (42 sc total)

RND 8: 3 sc, 1 inc [6 sc, 1 inc] 5 times, 3 sc (48 sc total)

RND 9: [7 sc, 1 inc] 6 times (54 sc total)

RND 10: 4 sc, 1 inc [8 sc, 1 inc] 5 times, 4 sc (60 sc total)

RND 11–15: 60 sc (5 rounds [60 sc in each round])

Change to Beige.

RND 16: In back loops only, 4 sc, 1 dec [8 sc, 1 dec] 5 times, 4 sc (54 sc total)

RND 17: [7 sc, 1 dec] 6 times (48 sc total)

Now it's time to embroider the mouth and attach the eyes. Embroider a mouth in the middle of round 13 using black embroidery floss.

Attach a pair of 4-mm safety eyes between rounds 12 and 13 with 5 st in between them.

RND 18: 3 sc, 1 dec [6 sc, 1 dec] 5 times, 3 sc (42 sc total)

RND 19: [5 sc, 1 dec] 6 times (36 sc total)

RND 20: 2 sc, 1 dec [4 sc, 1 dec] 5 times, 2 sc (30 sc total)

RND 21: [3 sc, 1 dec] 6 times (24 sc total)

Start stuffing, referring to the guide on page 11.

RND 22: 1 sc, 1 dec [2 sc, 1 dec] 5 times, 1 sc (18 sc total)

RND 23: [1 sc, 1 dec] 6 times (12 sc total)

RND 24: [1 dec] 6 times (6 sc total)

Cut yarn and fasten off all threads.

Embroider seeds on top of the Top Bun using your Beige yarn.

BOTTOM BUN

Using your Sand yarn, start with a magic ring.

RND 1: 6 sc into the ring (6 sc total)

RND 2: [1 inc] 6 times (12 sc total)

RND 3: [1 sc, 1 inc] 6 times (18 sc total)

RND 4: 1 sc, 1 inc [2 sc, 1 inc] 5 times, 1 sc (24 sc total)

RND 5: [3 sc, 1 inc] 6 times (30 sc total)

RND 6: 2 sc, 1 inc [4 sc, 1 inc] 5 times, 2 sc (36 sc total)

RND 7: [5 sc, 1 inc] 6 times (42 sc total)

RND 8: 3 sc, 1 inc [6 sc, 1 inc] 5 times, 3 sc (48 sc total)

RND 9: [7 sc, 1 inc] 6 times (54 sc total)

RND 10: 4 sc, 1 inc [8 sc, 1 inc] 5 times, 4 sc (60 sc total)

RND 11–13: 60 sc (3 rounds [60 sc in each round])

Change to Beige.

RND 14: In back loops only, 4 sc, 1 dec [8 sc, 1 dec] 5 times, 4 sc (54 sc total)

RND 15: [7 sc, 1 dec] 6 times (48 sc total)

RND 16: 3 sc, 1 dec [6 sc, 1 dec] 5 times, 3 sc (42 sc total)

RND 17: [5 sc, 1 dec] 6 times (36 sc total)

RND 18: 2 sc, 1 dec [4 sc, 1 dec] 5 times, 2 sc (30 sc total)

RND 19: [3 sc, 1 dec] 6 times (24 sc total)

Start stuffing, referring to the guide on page 11.

RND 20: 1 sc, 1 dec [2 sc, 1 dec] 5 times, 1 sc (18 sc total)

RND 21: [1 sc, 1 dec] 6 times (12 sc total)

RND 22: [1 dec] 6 times (6 sc total)

Cut yarn and fasten off all threads.

CHEEKS (MAKE 2)

Using your Pink yarn, start with a magic ring.

RND 1: 6 sc into the magic ring (6 sc total)

Finish with 1 sl.

Cut yarn but leave a long tail for sewing. Pin the Cheeks to the Top Bun and sew them on.

PATTY

Using your Brown yarn, start with a magic ring.

RND 1: 6 sc into the ring (6 sc total)

RND 2: [1 inc] 6 times (12 sc total)

RND 3: [1 sc, 1 inc] 6 times (18 sc total)

RND 4: 1 sc, 1 inc [2 sc, 1 inc] 5 times, 1 sc (24 sc total)

RND 5: [3 sc, 1 inc] 6 times (30 sc total)

RND 6: 2 sc, 1 inc [4 sc, 1 inc] 5 times, 2 sc (36 sc total)

RND 7: [5 sc, 1 inc] 6 times (42 sc total)

RND 8: 3 sc, 1 inc [6 sc, 1 inc] 5 times, 3 sc (48 sc total)

RND 9: [7 sc, 1 inc] 6 times (54 sc total)

RND 10: 4 sc, 1 inc [8 sc, 1 inc] 5 times, 4 sc (60 sc total)

RND 11: In back loops only, 60 sc (60 sc total)

RND 12: In back loops only, 4 sc, 1 dec [8 sc, 1 dec] 5 times, 4 sc (54 sc total)

RND 13: [7 sc, 1 dec] 6 times (48 sc total)

RND 14: 3 sc, 1 dec [6 sc, 1 dec] 5 times, 3 sc (42 sc total)

RND 15: [5 sc, 1 dec] 6 times (36 sc total)

RND 16: 2 sc, 1 dec [4 sc, 1 dec] 5 times, 2 sc (30 sc total)

RND 17: [3 sc, 1 dec] 6 times (24 sc total)

RND 18: 1 sc, 1 dec [2 sc, 1 dec] 5 times, 1 sc (18 sc total)

RND 19: [1 sc, 1 dec] 6 times (12 sc total)

RND 20: [1 dec] 6 times (6 sc total)

Cut yarn and fasten off all threads.

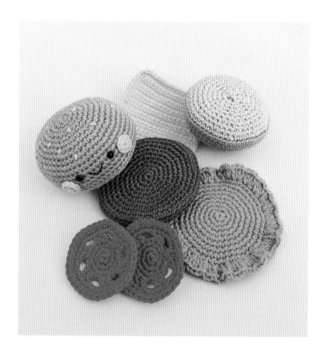

LETTUCE

Using your Green yarn, start with a magic ring.

RND 1: 6 sc into the ring (6 sc total)

RND 2: [1 inc] 6 times (12 sc total)

RND 3: [1 sc, 1 inc] 6 times (18 sc total)

RND 4: 1 sc, 1 inc [2 sc, 1 inc] 5 times, 1 sc (24 sc total)

RND 5: [3 sc, 1 inc] 6 times (30 sc total)

RND 6: 2 sc, 1 inc [4 sc, 1 inc] 5 times, 2 sc (36 sc total)

RND 7: [5 sc, 1 inc] 6 times (42 sc total)

RND 8: 3 sc, 1 inc [6 sc, 1 inc] 5 times, 3 sc (48 sc total)

RND 9: [7 sc, 1 inc] 6 times (54 sc total)

RND 10: 4 dc in the first st *skip 1 st, 4 dc in the next st*

Repeat from * to * for the entire round.

Finish with 1 sl.

CHEESE

Using your Yellow yarn, ch 18.

ROW 1: Starting in the second ch from the hook, 17 sc, ch 1 (does not count as st), and turn (17 sc total).

ROW 2–17: 17 sc and turn (16 rows [17 sc in each row])

Sc around the Cheese, working 2 sc in each corner.

Cut yarn and fasten off all threads.

TOMATOES (MAKE 2)

Using your Red yarn, start with a magic ring.

RND 1: 6 sc into the ring (6 sc total)

RND 2: [1 inc] 6 times (12 sc total)

RND 3: [1 sc, 1 inc] 6 times (18 sc total)

1 sl in next st.

RND 4: Ch 2 (counts as first dc), 1 dc, ch 3, skip 1 st, *2 dc, ch 3, skip 1 st*

Repeat from * to * for the entire round. (12 dc, 6 ch 3 spaces total)

RND 5: [2 sc, 3 sc into the ch 3 space] 6 times (30 sc total)

RND 6: [4 sc, 1 inc] 6 times (36 sc total)

Finish with 1 sl.

Cut yarn and fasten off all threads.

Fri-Day Fries

These Fri-Day Fries are a really fun and easy make! All you need are three colors of yarn, and no stuffing is required. You will start by making the box for your fries, and then you will make the fries themselves. This is another great project for children's play food (or just any fast food lover in your life!), since the fries can be taken out of the box and put in again.

SKILL LEVEL: BEGINNER

MATERIALS

Light fingering weight yarn in Hot Pink, Pink and Yellow

US B/1 (2.25-mm) hook

Tapestry needle

Black embroidery floss

A pair of 6-mm safety eyes

ABBREVIATIONS

rnd: round

ch: chain

sc: single crochet

1 inc: single crochet 2 stitches into the same stitch

1 dec: single crochet 2 stitches together

hdc: half double crochet

sl: slip stitch

st(s): stitch(es)

Approximate size for a finished Fri-Day Fries: 3.5 x 2.7 inches (9 x 7 cm)

Fri-Day Fries Pattern

BOX

Using your Hot Pink yarn, ch 15.

RND 1: Starting in the second ch from the hook, 13 sc, 3 sc in the next st, turn around the corner and working in the loops on the other side of the chain, 12 sc, 1 inc (30 sc total).

RND 2: 1 inc, 12 sc, [1 inc] 3 times, 12 sc, [1 inc] 2 times (36 sc total)

RND 3: 1 inc, 14 sc, [1 inc] 4 times, 14 sc, [1 inc] 3 times (44 sc total)

RND 4-17: 44 sc (14 rounds [14 sc in each round])

Finish with 3 sl.

Cut yarn and fasten off all threads.

Embroider a mouth in the middle of round 10 using black embroidery floss.

Attach a pair of 6-mm safety eyes between rounds 11 and 12 with 6 st in between them.

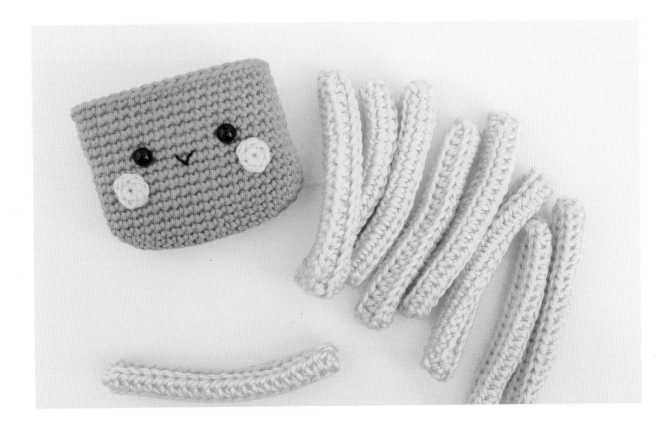

CHEEKS (MAKE 2)

Using your Pink yarn, start with a magic ring.

RND 1: 6 sc into the magic ring (6 sc total)

Finish with 1 sl.

Cut yarn but leave a long tail for sewing. Pin the Cheeks to the Box and sew them on.

FRIES (MAKE 9)

Using your Yellow yarn, ch 21.

ROW 1: Starting in the second ch from the hook, 20 hdc, ch 1 (does not count as st throughout), and turn (20 hdc total).

ROW 2: In back loops only, 20 hdc, ch 1 and turn (20 hdc total)

ROW 3: In front loops only, 20 hdc, ch 1 and turn (20 hdc total)

ROW 4: In back loops only, 20 hdc, ch 1 (20 hdc total)

Cut yarn but leave a long tail for sewing.

Sew the top of the Fries together, followed by the long side and then the bottom.

Sweet Treats

DESSERT DOLLS THAT ARE CUTE ENOUGH TO EAT!

Calling all sweet tooths! Here is the chapter for you. Whether you like cake, cupcakes or donuts, you'll be sure to find a pattern that satisfies every crochet craving.

Show some love to the people who matter most in your life by giving them a Love Lollipop (page 101), or celebrate your birthday any day of the year with a Rainbow Unicorn Cake (page 105). Crochet yourself a tray of Tasty Teddy Cupcakes (page 119) or stitch your worries away as you make the Donut Worry Turtle (page 115).

Love Lollipop

Here we have a Love Lollipop—a fun project that would make the perfect Valentine's Day gift. The heart is made in two colors, and after it's stuffed you crochet the runny frosting. Show someone special how much they mean to you with this lovely amigurumi!

SKILL LEVEL: INTERMEDIATE

MATERIALS

Light fingering weight yarn in Light Yellow, Hot Pink, Pink and Sand
US B/1 (2.25-mm) hook
Tapestry needle
A pair of 5-mm safety eyes
Black embroidery floss
Polyester stuffing
Small amounts of other yarn colors for sewing sprinkles

ABBREVIATIONS

rnd: round
ch: chain
sc: single crochet
1 inc: single crochet 2 stitches into the same stitch
1 dec: single crochet 2 stitches together
dc: double crochet
hdc: half double crochet
sl: slip stitch
st(s): stitch(es)

Approximate size for a finished Love Lollipop: 5 x 2.7 inches (13 x 7 cm)

Love Lollipop Pattern

TOP OF HEART (MAKE 2)

Using your Light Yellow yarn, start with a magic ring.

RND 1: 6 sc into the magic ring (6 sc total)

RND 2: [1 inc] 6 times (12 sc total)

RND 3: [1 sc, 1 inc] 6 times (18 sc total)

RND 4: 1 sc, 1 inc [2 sc, 1 inc] 5 times, 1 sc (24 sc total)

RND 5–7: 24 sc (3 rounds [24 sc in each round])

Cut the yarn on one of the pieces but leave a long yarn tail.

Do not cut the yarn on the second piece.

You are now going to crochet the two Tops together. For step-by-step photos of this process, see page 102.

Place Top 2 (the one that still has the yarn attached) beside Top 1 so you have them side-by-side.

Start crocheting in Top 1.

RND 1: 24 sc around each Top (48 sc total)

RND 2–4: 48 sc (3 rounds [48 sc in each round])

Sew the hole together between the two Tops using the yarn you saved from Top 1.

Place Top 1 and 2 next to each other.

Begin crocheting in Top 1.

Crochet 24 sc around each Top (48 sc total).

Sew the hole together between the two Tops.

After you have sewn the hole together, your piece should look like this.

RND 5: [6 sc, 1 dec] 6 times (42 sc total)

RND 6: 42 sc (42 sc total)

Change to Hot Pink.

RND 7: In back loops only, [5 sc, 1 dec] 6 times (36 sc total)

RND 8: 36 sc (36 sc total)

Now it's time to attach the safety eyes. Attach a pair of 5-mm safety eyes between rounds 3 and 4 with 7 st between them. Embroider a mouth in the middle of round 5 using black embroidery floss.

RND 9: [4 sc, 1 dec] 6 times (30 sc total)

RND 10: 30 sc (30 sc total)

Start stuffing, referring to the guide on page 11.

RND 11: [3 sc, 1 dec] 6 times (24 sc total)

RND 12: 24 sc (24 sc total)

RND 13: [2 sc, 1 dec] 6 times (18 sc total)

RND 14: 18 sc (18 sc total)

RND 15: [1 sc, 1 dec] 6 times (12 sc total)

RND 16: [1 dec] 6 times (6 sc total)

Cut yarn and fasten off all threads.

RUNNY FROSTING

Using your Light Yellow yarn, rejoin in one of the front loops of round 7 on the Top.

In remaining front loops of round 7, *1 sc, 1 hdc, 2 dc, 1 hdc, 1 sc, 2 sl, 1 sc, 2 dc, 1 sc, 2 sl*

Repeat from * to * 2 more times.

Cut yarn and fasten off all threads.

CHEEKS (MAKE 2)

Using your Pink yarn, start with a magic ring.

RND 1: 6 sc into the magic ring (6 sc total)

Finish with 1 sl.

Cut your yarn but leave a long tail for sewing. Pin the Cheeks to the Lollipop and sew them on.

Embroider sprinkles in different colors.

STICK

Using your Sand yarn, start with a magic ring.

RND 1: 6 sc into the magic ring (6 sc total)

Start stuffing once you have worked a few rounds, and keep stuffing a little at a time as you crochet more rounds.

RND 2–18: 6 sc (17 rounds, [6 sc in each round])

Finish with 1 sl.

Cut your yarn but leave a long tail for sewing.

Pin the Stick to the bottom of the Lollipop and sew it on.

Rainbow Unicorn Cake

Cake + rainbow + unicorn = the perfect cake! The cake is made in separate pieces that you sew together using white sewing thread to make the seams more invisible. You will also add a small piece of cardboard in the bottom to make it stand upright and to give it a nice, flat surface. Perfect for any party, this colorful cake is sure to brighten anyone's day!

SKILL LEVEL: INTERMEDIATE

MATERIALS

Light fingering weight yarn in White, Sand, Purple, Blue, Green, Yellow, Orange, Hot Pink, Pink and Gray

US B/1 (2.25-mm) hook

A small piece of cardboard

A pair of 6-mm safety eyes

Tapestry needle

Black embroidery floss

White sewing thread

Polyester stuffing

Small amounts of other yarn colors for sewing sprinkles

ABBREVIATIONS

rnd: round

ch: chain

sc: single crochet

1 inc: single crochet 2 stitches into the same stitch

1 dec: single crochet 2 stitches together

dc: double crochet

sl: slip stitch

st(s): stitch(es)

Approximate size for a finished Rainbow Unicorn Cake: 4 x 2.3 inches (10 x 6 cm)

Rainbow Unicorn Cake Pattern

CAKE FROSTING

Using your White yarn, ch 17.

CAKE END

ROW 1: Starting in the second ch from the hook, 16 sc, ch 1 (does not count as st throughout), and turn (16 sc total).

ROW 2–12: 16 sc, ch 1 and turn (11 rows, [16 sc in each row])

CAKE TOP

ROW 13: In back loops only, 16 sc, ch 1 and turn (16 sc total)

ROW 14–16: 16 sc, ch 1 and turn (3 rows, [16 sc in each row])

ROW 17: 1 dec, 12 sc, 1 dec, ch 1 and turn (14 sc total)

ROW 18–19: 14 sc, ch 1 and turn (2 rows, [14 sc in each row])

ROW 20: 1 dec, 10 sc, 1 dec, ch 1 and turn (12 sc total)

ROW 21–22: 12 sc, ch 1 and turn (2 rows, [12 sc in each row])

ROW 23: 1 dec, 8 sc, 1 dec, ch 1 and turn (10 sc total)

ROW 24–25: 10 sc, ch 1 and turn (2 rows, [10 sc in each row])

ROW 26: 1 dec, 6 sc, 1 dec, ch 1 and turn (8 sc total)

ROW 27–28: 8 sc, ch 1 and turn (2 rows, [8 sc in each row])

ROW 29: 1 dec, 4 sc, 1 dec, ch 1 and turn (6 sc total)

ROW 30–31: 6 sc, ch 1 and turn (2 rows, [6 sc in each row])

ROW 32: 1 dec, 2 sc, 1 dec, ch 1 and turn (4 sc total)

ROW 33–34: 4 sc, ch 1 and turn (2 rows, [4 sc in each row])

ROW 35: [1 dec] 2 times, ch 1 and turn (2 sc total)

ROW 36: 1 dec (1 sc total)

Ch 1 and turn. Now you are going to sc around the Cake Frosting. Work 36 sc along the first long side, 16 sc along the short side and 36 sc along the second long side.

Finish with 1 sl in the first sc.

Cut yarn and fasten off all threads.

CAKE BOTTOM

Using your Sand yarn, ch 17.

ROW 1: Starting in the second ch from the hook, 16 sc, ch 1, and turn. (16 sc total)

ROW 2–4: 16 sc, ch 1 and turn (3 rows, [16 sc in each row])

ROW 5: 1 dec, 12 sc, 1 dec, ch 1 and turn (14 sc total)

ROW 6–7: 14 sc, ch 1 and turn (2 rows, [14 sc in each row])

ROW 8: 1 dec, 10 sc, 1 dec, ch 1 and turn (12 sc total)

ROW 9–10: 12 sc, ch 1 and turn (2 rows, [12 sc in each row])

ROW 11: 1 dec, 8 sc, 1 dec, ch 1 and turn (10 sc total)

ROW 12–13: 10 sc, ch 1 and turn (2 rows, [10 sc in each row])

ROW 14: 1 dec, 6 sc, 1 dec, ch 1 and turn (8 sc total)

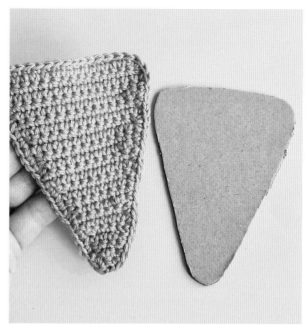

Place your work on a piece of cardboard and cut out a piece that's the same size as the bottom.

ROW 15–16: 8 sc, ch 1 and turn (2 rows, [8 sc in each row])

ROW 17: 1 dec, 4 sc, 1 dec, ch 1 and turn (6 sc total)

ROW 18–19: 6 sc, ch 1 and turn (2 rows, [6 sc in each row])

ROW 20: 1 dec, 2 sc, 1 dec, ch 1 and turn (4 sc total)

ROW 21–22: 4 sc, ch 1 and turn (2 rows, [4 sc in each row])

ROW 23: [1 dec] 2 times, ch 1 and turn (2 sc total)

ROW 24: 1 dec (1 sc total)

Ch 1 and turn. Now you are going to sc around the Cake Bottom. Work 24 sc along the first long side, 16 sc along the short side and 24 sc along the second long side.

Finish with 1 sl in the first sc.

Cut yarn and fasten off all threads.

Place your work on a piece of cardboard and cut out a piece that's the same size as the bottom. You are going to place the cardboard piece in the bottom of the cake later. This will give more stability to your Rainbow Unicorn Cake.

RAINBOW SIDES (MAKE 2)

Using your Purple yarn, ch 25.

ROW 1: Starting in the second ch from the hook, 24 sc (24 sc total)

ROW 2: 24 sc, ch 1 and turn (24 sc total)

Change to Blue.

ROW 3–4: 24 sc, ch 1 and turn (2 rows, [24 sc in each row])

Change to Green.

ROW 5–6: 24 sc, ch 1 and turn (2 rows, [24 sc in each row])

Change to Yellow.

ROW 7–8: 24 sc, ch 1 and turn (2 rows, [24 sc in each row])

Change to Orange.

ROW 9–10: 24 sc, ch 1 and turn (2 rows, [24 sc in each row])

Change to Hot Pink.

ROW 11–12: 24 sc, ch 1 and turn (2 rows, [24 sc in each row])

Cut yarn and fasten off all threads.

Now you will attach the safety eyes and embroider a mouth onto one of the Rainbow Sides.

Embroider a mouth in the middle of round 6 using black embroidery floss, then attach a pair of 6-mm safety eyes between rounds 7 and 8 with 5 st between them.

CHEEKS (MAKE 2)

Using your Pink yarn, start with a magic ring.

RND 1: 6 sc into the magic ring.

Finish with 1 sl.

Cut your yarn but leave a long tail for sewing. Pin the Cheeks to the Rainbow Side with the mouth and eyes and sew them on.

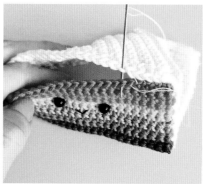

Start by sewing the short side of the Rainbow Side to the end of the Cake Frosting.

Continue to sew it along the long side to the top of the Frosting.

Sew the two Rainbow Sides together at the front.

Sew on the Cake Bottom.

Make sure the piece of cardboard is placed on top of the Cake Bottom before you finish stuffing and sewing your Cake.

Now it's time to sew the Cake together!

Using your white sewing thread, start by sewing the short side of the Rainbow Side (the side with the face) to the end of the Cake Frosting. Continue to sew it along the long side to the top of the Frosting.

When you have sewn one of the Rainbow Sides, repeat this step with the other side. Then sew the two Rainbow Sides together at the front.

Last, sew the Cake Bottom, with the cardboard placed on top, to your Cake.

Don't forget to stuff your Cake before you sew on the Bottom completely.

DECORATIVE FROSTING

Hold your Cake with the pointy end facing toward you.

Using your White yarn, you are going to crochet in the free loops of row 13 on the top of the Cake Frosting.

4 dc in the first st, [2 sl, 4 dc in the next st] 4 times, 3 sl

Cut yarn and fasten off all threads.

Embroider sprinkles in different colors on top of your Rainbow Unicorn Cake.

UNICORN HORN

Using your Gray yarn, start with a magic ring.

RND 1: 6 sc into the magic ring (6 sc total)

RND 2: 6 sc (6 sc total)

RND 3: [1 sc, 1 inc] 3 times (9 sc total)

RND 4-6: 9 sc (3 rounds, [9 sc in each round])

Cut yarn but leave a long tail for sewing.

Stuff the Horn a little bit and pin it on top of your Cake. Sew it on.

Delicious Ice Cream

This delicious bowl of ice cream is such a fun make! First you will make the bowl, then you put the ice cream with topping inside it. Make sure to have fun with the colors in this project—if you're not a fan of strawberry ice cream, why not make a chocolate, vanilla or mint version?

SKILL LEVEL: INTERMEDIATE

MATERIALS

Light fingering weight yarn in Light Blue, Pink, Hot Pink, White, Red and Green
US B/1 (2.25-mm) hook
A small piece of cardboard
Polyester stuffing
Tapestry needle
Black embroidery floss
A pair of 6-mm safety eyes
Small amounts of other yarn colors for sewing sprinkles
White sewing thread

ABBREVIATIONS

rnd: round
ch: chain
sc: single crochet
1 inc: single crochet 2 stitches into the same stitch
1 dec: single crochet 2 stitches together
hdc: half double crochet
sl: slip stitch
st(s): stitch(es)

Approximate size for a finished Delicious Ice Cream:
6 x 2.7 inches (15 x 7 cm)

Delicious Ice Cream Pattern

BOWL

Using your Light Blue yarn, start with a magic ring.

RND 1: 6 sc into the ring (6 sc total)

RND 2: [1 inc] 6 times (12 sc total)

RND 3: [1 sc, 1 inc] 6 times (18 sc total)

RND 4: 1 sc, 1 inc [2 sc, 1 inc] 5 times, 1 sc (24 sc total)

RND 5: [3 sc, 1 inc] 6 times (30 sc total)

RND 6: 2 sc, 1 inc [4 sc, 1 inc] 5 times, 2 sc (36 sc total)

RND 7: [5 sc, 1 inc] 6 times (42 sc total)

RND 8: 3 sc, 1 inc [6 sc, 1 inc] 5 times, 3 sc (48 sc total)

RND 9–10: 48 sc (2 rounds, [48 sc in each round])

Put your work on a piece of cardboard and cut out a piece that's the same size as the bottom. Place the cardboard piece in the bottom of the Bowl. This will give more stability to your Delicious Ice Cream.

RND 11: 3 sc, 1 dec [6 sc, 1 dec] 5 times, 3 sc (42 sc total)

RND 28: 3 sc, 1 inc [6 sc, 1 inc] 5 times, 3 sc (48 sc total)

RND 29: [7 sc, 1 inc] 6 times (54 sc total)

RND 30–33: 54 sc (4 rounds, [54 sc in each round])

RND 34: 4 sc in the first st, *skip 1 st, 1 sl, skip 1 st, 4 sc in the next st*

Repeat from * to * for the entire round, finishing with skip 1 st, sl in first sc.

Cut yarn and fasten off all threads.

ICE CREAM

Using your Pink yarn, start with a magic ring.

RND 1: 6 sc into the ring (6 sc total)

RND 2: [1 inc] 6 times (12 sc total)

RND 3: [1 sc, 1 inc] 6 times (18 sc total)

RND 4: 1 sc, 1 inc [2 sc, 1 inc] 5 times, 1 sc (24 sc total)

RND 5: [3 sc, 1 inc] 6 times (30 sc total)

RND 6: 2 sc, 1 inc [4 sc, 1 inc] 5 times, 2 sc (36 sc total)

RND 7: [5 sc, 1 inc] 6 times (42 sc total)

RND 8: 3 sc, 1 inc [6 sc, 1 inc] 5 times, 3 sc (48 sc total)

RND 9–18: 48 sc (10 rounds, [48 sc in each round])

Now it's time to make the face. Embroider a mouth in the middle of round 12 using black embroidery floss.

Attach a pair of 6-mm safety eyes between rounds 11 and 12 with 6 st between them.

RND 19: 3 sc, 1 dec [6 sc, 1 dec] 5 times, 3 sc (42 sc total)

RND 20: [5 sc, 1 dec] 6 times (36 sc total)

RND 21: 2 sc, 1 dec [4 sc, 1 dec] 5 times, 2 sc (30 sc total)

Start stuffing, referring to the guide on page 11.

RND 22: [3 sc, 1 dec] 6 times (24 sc total)

RND 12: [5 sc, 1 dec] 6 times (36 sc total)

RND 13: 36 sc (36 sc total)

RND 14: 1 sc, 1 dec [4 sc, 1 dec] 5 times, 1 sc (30 sc total)

RND 15: [3 sc, 1 dec] 6 times (24 sc total)

RND 16: 24 sc (24 sc total)

Start stuffing; please note that you are only going to stuff into the bottom of the Bowl up to round 22.

RND 17: 1 sc, 1 dec [2 sc, 1 dec] 5 times, 1 sc (18 sc total)

RND 18: [1 sc, 1 dec] 6 times (12 sc total)

RND 19–22: 12 sc (4 rounds, [12 sc in each round])

RND 23: [1 sc, 1 inc] 6 times (18 sc total)

RND 24: 1 sc, 1 inc [2 sc, 1 inc] 5 times, 1 sc (24 sc total)

RND 25: [3 sc, 1 inc] 6 times (30 sc total)

RND 26: 2 sc, 1 inc [4 sc, 1 inc] 5 times, 2 sc (36 sc total)

RND 27: [5 sc, 1 inc] 6 times (42 sc total)

RND 23: 1 sc, 1 dec [2 sc, 1 dec] 5 times, 1 sc (18 sc total)

RND 24: [1 sc, 1 dec] 6 times (12 sc total)

RND 25: [1 dec] 6 times (6 sc total)

Cut yarn and fasten off all threads.

Embroider sprinkles in different colors onto the Ice Cream.

CHEEKS (MAKE 2)

Using your Hot Pink yarn, start with a magic ring.

RND 1: 6 sc into the magic ring.

Finish with 1 sl.

Cut your yarn but leave a long tail for sewing. Pin the Cheeks to the Ice Cream and sew them on.

WHIPPED CREAM

Using your White yarn, start with a magic ring.

RND 1: 6 sc into the magic ring (6 sc total)

RND 2: In back loops only, [1 inc] 6 times (12 sc total)

RND 3: In back loops only, [1 sc, 1 inc] 6 times (18 sc total)

RND 4: In back loops only, [2 sc, 1 inc] 6 times (24 sc total)

RND 5: In back loops only, [3 sc, 1 inc] 6 times (30 sc total)

Ch 1 (does not count as st), turn your work around and work 1 hdc in each front loop of round 5. (30 hdc total)

Continue with 1 hdc in each of the remaining loops all the way up to the top of the Whipped Cream.

Cut yarn but leave a long tail for sewing. Pin the Whipped Cream to the top of the Ice Cream and sew it on.

Turn your work around. You are now going to work in each front loop of Rnd 5.

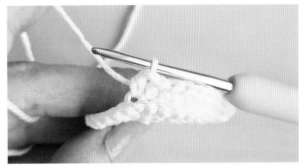

Work 1 hdc in each front loop of Rnd 5.

Continue with 1 hdc in each of the remaining loops all the way up to the top.

And your Whipped Cream is done!

CHERRY

Using your Red yarn, start with a magic ring.

RND 1: 6 sc into the magic ring (6 sc total)

RND 2: [1 inc] 6 times (12 sc total)

RND 3–5: 12 sc (3 rounds, [12 sc in each round])

Stuff your Cherry.

RND 6: [1 dec] 6 times (6 sc total)

Cut yarn and fasten off all threads.

CHERRY STEM

Using your Green yarn, ch 3.

RND 1: Starting in the second ch from the hook, 2 sc (2 sc total)

Cut yarn but leave a long tail for sewing.

Pin the Stem on top of the Cherry and sew it on.

Pin the Cherry on top of the Whipped Cream and sew it on using white sewing thread.

Place your Ice Cream into the Bowl and secure it with some stitches using your white sewing thread.

Donut Worry Turtle

If I were a turtle, I would for sure want to have a donut as a shell! The donut is made first, then you make the small turtle pieces and sew them onto it. Let your worries melt away as you stitch this fun project!

SKILL LEVEL: INTERMEDIATE

MATERIALS

Light fingering weight yarn in Sand,
Lilac, Green and Pink
US B/1 (2.25-mm) hook
Tapestry needle
Small amounts of other colors for sewing sprinkles
Polyester stuffing
A pair of 4-mm safety eyes
Black embroidery floss

ABBREVIATIONS

rnd: round
ch: chain
sc: single crochet
1 inc: single crochet 2 stitches into the same stitch
1 dec: single crochet 2 stitches together
dc: double crochet
sl: slip stitch
st(s): stitch(es)

Approximate size for a finished Donut Worry Turtle: 4 x 2.7 inches (10 x 7 cm)

Donut Worry Turtle Pattern

DONUT

Using your Sand yarn, ch 18, join with 1 sl to the first ch to make a ring.

RND 1–2: 18 sc into the ring (2 rounds, [18 sc in each round])

Change to Lilac.

RND 3–4: 18 sc (2 rounds, [18 sc in each round])

RND 5: 1 sc, 1 inc [2 sc, 1 inc] 5 times, 1 sc (24 sc total)

RND 6: [3 sc, 1 inc] 6 times (30 sc total)

RND 7: 2 sc, 1 inc [4 sc, 1 inc] 5 times, 2 sc (36 sc total)

RND 8: [5 sc, 1 inc] 6 times (42 sc total)

RND 9: 3 sc, 1 inc [6 sc, 1 inc] 5 times, 3 sc (48 sc total)

RND 10: [7 sc, 1 inc] 6 times (54 sc total)

RND 11: 4 sc, 1 inc [8 sc, 1 inc] 5 times, 4 sc (60 sc total)

RND 12–13: 60 sc (2 rounds, [60 sc in each round])

Change to Sand.

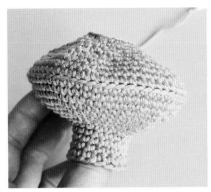

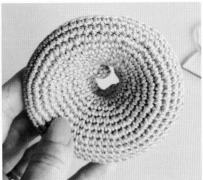

After Rnd 22, your piece should look like this.

Fold Rnds 1 to 4 into the inside of the Donut.

Begin to sew the Donut together.

RND 14: In back loops only, 60 sc (60 sc total)

RND 15: 60 sc (60 sc total)

RND 16: 4 sc, 1 dec [8 sc, 1 dec] 5 times, 4 sc (54 sc total)

RND 17: [7 sc, 1 dec] 6 times (48 sc total)

RND 18: 3 sc, 1 dec [6 sc, 1 dec] 5 times, 3 sc (42 sc total)

RND 19: [5 sc, 1 dec] 6 times (36 sc total)

RND 20: 2 sc, 1 dec [4 sc, 1 dec] 5 times, 2 sc (30 sc total)

RND 21: [3 sc, 1 dec] 6 times (24 sc total)

RND 22: 1 sc, 1 dec [2 sc, 1 dec] 5 times, 1 sc (18 sc total)

Finish with 1 sl.

Cut the yarn but leave a long yarn tail for sewing.

Begin to sew the Donut together, making sure to stuff it before you finish sewing.

RUNNY FROSTING

Using your Lilac yarn, rejoin in one of the front loops of round 13 on the Donut.

In remaining front loops of round 13, *4 sc in the next st, 3 sl, 2 sc in the next st, 3 sl*

Repeat from * to * for the entire round, omitting the last 2 sc and 3 sl on the final repeat.

Finish with 1 sl in the first sc.

Cut yarn and fasten off all threads.

Embroider sprinkles onto your Donut using yarn in different colors.

LEGS (MAKE 4)

Using your Green yarn, start with a magic ring.

RND 1: 5 sc into the magic ring (5 sc total)

RND 2: [1 inc] 5 times (10 sc total)

RND 3–4: 10 sc (2 rounds, [10 sc in each round])

Finish with 1 sl.

Cut yarn but leave a long tail for sewing.

Stuff the Legs and pin them to the Donut, then sew them on.

TAIL

Using your Green yarn, ch 5.

RND 1: Starting in the second ch from the hook, 4 sc (4 sc total)

Cut yarn but leave a long tail for sewing.

Pin the Tail to the back of the Donut and sew it on.

HEAD

Using your Green yarn, start with a magic ring.

RND 1: 6 sc into the ring (6 sc total)

RND 2: [1 inc] 6 times (12 sc total)

RND 3: [1 sc, 1 inc] 6 times (18 sc total)

RND 4: 1 sc, 1 inc [2 sc, 1 inc] 5 times, 1 sc (24 sc total)

RND 5–10: 24 sc (6 rounds, [24 sc in each round])

RND 11: 1 sc, 1 dec [2 sc, 1 dec] 5 times, 1 sc (18 sc total)

RND 12: 1 inc, 7 sc, 1 dec, 8 sc (18 sc total)

RND 13: 1 sc, 1 inc, 7 sc, 1 dec, 7 sc (18 sc total)

Now it's time to attach the safety eyes. Make sure that you place them at the front of the Head, which is where you made the decreases in the previous rounds. Attach a pair of 4-mm safety eyes between rounds 6 and 7 with 4 st between them.

Embroider a mouth in the middle of round 8 using black embroidery floss, then embroider cheeks using your Pink yarn.

RND 14: 1 sc, 1 inc, 7 sc, 1 dec, 7 sc (18 sc total)

RND 15: 2 sc, 1 inc, 7 sc, 1 dec, 6 sc (18 sc total)

Start stuffing, referring to the guide on page 11.

RND 16: [1 sc, 1 dec] 6 times (12 sc total)

RND 17: [1 dec] 6 times (6 sc total)

Cut yarn but leave a long tail for sewing.

Pin the Head to the Donut and sew it on.

Tasty Teddy Cupcake

This Tasty Teddy Cupcake is made in separate pieces. First you will make the cupcake base, then you'll make the teddy. Why not make a variety of adorable animals? Just switch out the ears for the Charming Bunny Cactus (page 140) ears or the Magical Unicorn Popsicle (page 15) ears and horn for a whole tray of cupcake creatures!

SKILL LEVEL: INTERMEDIATE

MATERIALS

Light fingering weight yarn in Mint, Lilac, Brown, Hot Pink, Pink, White, Red and Green

US B/1 (2.25-mm) hook

A small piece of cardboard

Tapestry needle

Black embroidery floss

A pair of 6-mm safety eyes

Polyester stuffing

Red sewing thread

ABBREVIATIONS

rnd: round

ch: chain

sc: single crochet

1 inc: single crochet 2 stitches into the same stitch

1 dec: single crochet 2 stitches together

sl: slip stitch

st(s): stitch(es)

Approximate size for a finished Tasty Teddy Cupcake: 4.3 x 3.5 inches (11 x 9 cm)

Tasty Teddy Cupcake Pattern

CUPCAKE BASE

Using your Mint yarn, start with a magic ring.

RND 1: 6 sc into the magic ring (6 sc total)

RND 2: [1 inc] 6 times (12 sc total)

RND 3: [1 sc, 1 inc] 6 times (18 sc total)

RND 4: 1 sc, 1 inc [2 sc, 1 inc] 5 times, 1 sc (24 sc total)

RND 5: [3 sc, 1 inc] 6 times (30 sc total)

RND 6: 2 sc, 1 inc [4 sc, 1 inc] 5 times, 2 sc (36 sc total)

RND 7: In back loops only, 36 sc (36 sc total)

Change to Lilac.

RND 8: 36 sc (36 sc total)

Change to Mint.

RND 9: [5 sc, 1 in] 6 times (42 sc total)

Change to Lilac.

RND 10: 42 sc (42 sc total)

Change to Mint.

RND 11: 42 sc (42 sc total)

Change to Lilac.

RND 12: 42 sc (42 sc total)

Change to Mint.

RND 13: 3 sc, 1 inc [6 sc, 1 inc] 5 times, 3 sc (48 sc total)

Change to Lilac.

RND 14: 48 sc (48 sc total)

Change to Mint.

RND 15: 48 sc (48 sc total)

Change to Lilac.

RND 16: 48 sc (48 sc total)

Finish with 1 sl. Cut yarn and fasten off all threads.

Put your work on a piece of cardboard and cut out a piece that's the same size as the bottom. Place the cardboard piece in the bottom of the Cupcake Base. This will give more stability to your Cupcake.

TEDDY BEAR

Using your Brown yarn, start with a magic ring.

RND 1: 6 sc into the ring (6 sc total)

RND 2: [1 inc] 6 times (12 sc total)

RND 3: [1 sc, 1 inc] 6 times (18 sc total)

RND 4: 1 sc, 1 inc [2 sc, 1 inc] 5 times, 1 sc (24 sc total)

RND 5: [3 sc, 1 inc] 6 times (30 sc total)

RND 6: 2 sc, 1 inc [4 sc, 1 inc] 5 times, 2 sc (36 sc total)

RND 7: [5 sc, 1 inc] 6 times (42 sc total)

RND 8: 3 sc, 1 inc [6 sc, 1 inc] 5 times, 3 sc (48 sc total)

RND 9–17: 48 sc (9 rounds [48 sc in each round])

Finish with 1 sl.

Cut yarn but leave a long tail for sewing.

Now it's time for the face! Embroider a nose between rounds 12 and 13 using Hot Pink yarn and black embroidery floss.

Attach a pair of 6-mm safety eyes between rounds 11 and 12 with 5 st between them.

Begin sewing the Teddy Bear on top of the Cupcake Base. When you're part of the way through sewing, start to stuff your Tasty Teddy Cupcake.

CHEEKS (MAKE 2)

Using your Pink yarn, start with a magic ring.

RND 1: 6 sc into the magic ring

Finish with 1 sl.

Cut your yarn but leave a long tail for sewing. Pin the Cheeks to the Tasty Teddy Cupcake and sew them on.

EARS (MAKE 2)

Using your Brown yarn, start with a magic ring.

RND 1: 6 sc into the ring (6 sc total)

RND 2: [1 inc] 6 times (12 sc total)

RND 3: 12 sc (12 sc total)

RND 4: [1 sc, 1 inc] 6 times (18 sc total)

RND 5–8: 18 sc (4 rounds [18 sc in each round])

RND 9: [1 sc, 1 dec] 6 times (12 sc total)

Cut the yarn but leave a long yarn tail for sewing.

Press the Ear flat with your hands, if necessary.

INSIDE THE EAR (MAKE 2)

Using your Hot Pink yarn, start with a magic ring.

RND 1: 6 sc into the ring (6 sc total)

RND 2: [1 inc] 6 times (12 sc total)

Finish with 3 sl.

Cut yarn but leave a long tail for sewing.

Pin the inside of the Ear onto the main Ear piece and sew it on.

Pin the Ears to your Tasty Teddy Cupcake and sew them on.

FEET (MAKE 2)

Using your Brown yarn, start with a magic ring.

RND 1: 6 sc into the ring (6 sc total)

RND 2: [1 inc] 6 times (12 sc total)

RND 3: [1 sc, 1 inc] 6 times (18 sc total)

RND 4: 7 sc, [1 dec] 2 times, 7 sc (16 sc total)

RND 5: 6 sc, [1 dec] 2 times, 6 sc (14 sc total)

Finish with 1 sl.

Cut yarn but leave a long tail for sewing.

Stuff the Feet and pin them to your Tasty Teddy Cupcake and sew them on.

ARMS (MAKE 2)

Using your Brown yarn, start with a magic ring.

RND 1: 6 sc into the ring (6 sc total)

RND 2–5: 6 sc (4 rounds [6 sc in each round])

Finish with 1 sl.

Cut yarn but leave a long tail for sewing.

Pin the Arms to your Tasty Teddy Cupcake and sew them on.

WHIPPED CREAM

Using your White yarn, start with a magic ring.

RND 1: 6 sc into the magic ring (6 sc total)

RND 2: [1 inc] 6 times (12 sc total)

RND 3: [1 sc, 1 inc] 6 times (18 sc total)

RND 4: In front loops only, 4 sc in each st around

Cut yarn but leave a long tail for sewing.

Pin the Whipped Cream on top of your Tasty Teddy Cupcake and sew it on.

STRAWBERRY

Using your Red yarn, start with a magic ring.

RND 1: 6 sc into the magic ring (6 sc total)

RND 2: 6 sc (6 sc total)

RND 3: [1 inc] 6 times (12 sc total)

RND 4–5: 12 sc (2 rounds, [12 sc in each round])

Start stuffing your Strawberry.

RND 6: In back loops only, [1 dec] 6 times (6 sc total)

Sew the hole together and fasten off.

STRAWBERRY LEAVES

Using your Green yarn, start with a magic ring, but don't pull it together.

Ch 3, 1 sc in the second ch from the hook, 1 sc, 1 sl into the ring

Repeat from * to * 4 more times to create 5 Leaves. Pull the magic ring closed.

Cut your yarn but leave a long tail for sewing. Sew the Leaves onto the Strawberry.

Pin the Strawberry on top of your Tasty Teddy Cupcake and sew it on using your red sewing thread.

Cactus Makes Perfect

SMILING SUCCULENTS AND OTHER PLANT PROJECTS

Do you struggle to keep real plants alive? Not to worry—the plants in this book require no water or sunshine. Create the indoor garden of your dreams that will stay looking cute and lively forever! In this chapter, you will find beginner-friendly patterns and a few intermediate patterns as well.

The Sweet Succulent Family (page 127) incorporates some nice color-changing in the plant pot, providing a great opportunity for beginners to practice their color-changing skills! Or maybe you have a dinner party to go to but have no flowers for the host? The Cute & Cuddly Cactus (page 132) is a quick make that works up easily. Whip one up in an afternoon and you'll have the perfect gift!

My favorite pattern in this chapter is the Cheeky Unicorn Cactus (page 137), because—you guessed it—it's a unicorn and a cactus together! While I may be obsessed with all things unicorn, if that's not your thing you should feel more than free to turn this cactus into another animal, or just skip the animal part altogether. Your cactus creation will be looking sharp either way!

Sweet Succulent Family

Get ready to craft a cute little family of succulents! The pot for these succulents is a bit bigger than the rest of the cacti in this chapter, because you'll need to fit a whole family in it. After you have made your pot, you will crochet each cactus separately. And if you sew them even more closely together, you can fit a second baby into the pot if you'd like. Crochet the day away with the cutest cacti family you've ever seen!

SKILL LEVEL: INTERMEDIATE

MATERIALS

Light fingering weight yarn in Light Red, Light Yellow, Brown, Green and Pink
US B/1 (2.25-mm) hook
A small piece of cardboard
Polyester stuffing
Tapestry needle
Black embroidery floss
Two pairs of 5-mm safety eyes
One pair of 4-mm safety eyes

ABBREVIATIONS

rnd: round
ch: chain
sc: single crochet
1 inc: single crochet 2 stitches into the same stitch
1 dec: single crochet 2 stitches together
sl: slip stitch
st(s): stitch(es)

Approximate size for a finished Sweet Succulent Family: 4.7 x 4.3 inches (12 x 11 cm)

Sweet Succulent Family Pattern

POT

Using your Light Red yarn, start with a magic ring.

RND 1: 6 sc into the magic ring (6 sc total)

RND 2: [1 inc] 6 times (12 sc total)

RND 3: [1 sc, 1 inc] 6 times (18 sc total)

RND 4: 1 sc, 1 inc [2 sc, 1 inc] 5 times, 1 sc (24 sc total)

RND 5: [3 sc, 1 inc] 6 times (30 sc total)

RND 6: 2 sc, 1 inc [4 sc, 1 inc] 5 times, 2 sc (36 sc total)

RND 7: [5 sc, 1 inc] 6 times (42 sc total)

RND 8: 3 sc, 1 inc [6 sc, 1 inc] 5 times, 3 sc (48 sc total)

RND 9: In back loops only, 48 sc (48 sc total)

RND 10: 48 sc (48 sc total)

RND 11: [7 sc, 1 inc] 6 times (54 sc total)

RND 12: 54 sc (54 sc total)

RND 13: *1 sc in Light Yellow, 1 sc in Light Red*

Repeat from * to * for the entire round (54 sc total).

Color Changing Step 1: Work the last stitch until you have 2 loops left on your hook, change to Light Yellow and pull it through.

Repeat Color Changing Step 1, but change to Light Red when you have 2 loops left.

Repeat the Color Changing steps for the entire Rnd.

And here is how pretty it looks!

RND 14: With Light Red only, 4 sc, 1 inc [8 sc, 1 inc] 5 times, 4 sc (60 sc total)

RND 15–16: 60 sc (2 rounds, [60 sc in each round])

RND 17: [9 sc, 1 inc] 6 times (66 sc total)

RND 18: 66 sc (66 sc total)

RND 19: *1 sc in Light Yellow, 1 sc in Light Red*

Repeat from * to * for the entire round (66 sc total).

RND 20–22: With Light Red only, 66 sc (3 rounds, [66 sc in each round])

RND 23: [9 sc, 1 dec] 6 times (60 sc total)

RND 24: In front loops only, 60 sc (60 sc total)

RND 25: 60 sc (60 sc total)

Finish with 1 sl.

Cut yarn and fasten off all threads.

Put your work on a piece of cardboard and cut out a piece that's the same size as the bottom. Place the cardboard piece in the bottom of the Pot. This will give more stability to your succulent Pot.

SOIL

Using your Brown yarn, rejoin in one of the back loops of round 24 on the Pot.

RND 1: In remaining back loops of round 24, 4 sc, 1 dec [8 sc, 1 dec] 5 times, 4 sc (54 sc total)

RND 2: [7 sc, 1 dec] 6 times (48 sc total)

RND 3: 3 sc, 1 dec [6 sc, 1 dec] 5 times, 3 sc (42 sc total)

RND 4: [5 sc, 1 dec] 6 times (36 sc total)

RND 5: 2 sc, 1 dec [4 sc, 1 dec] 5 times, 2 sc (30 sc total)

Start stuffing, referring to the guide on page 11.

RND 6: [3 sc, 1 dec] 6 times (24 sc total)

RND 7: 1 sc, 1 dec [2 sc, 1 dec] 5 times, 1 sc (18 sc total)

RND 8: [1 sc, 1 dec] 6 times (12 sc total)

RND 9: [1 dec] 6 times (6 sc total)

Cut yarn and fasten off all threads.

DADDY SUCCULENT

Using your Green yarn, start with a magic ring.

RND 1: 6 sc into the magic ring (6 sc total)

RND 2: [1 inc] 6 times (12 sc total)

RND 3: [1 sc, 1 inc] 6 times (18 sc total)

RND 4: 1 sc, 1 inc [2 sc, 1 inc] 5 times, 1 sc (24 sc total)

RND 5: [3 sc, 1 inc] 6 times (30 sc total)

RND 6: 30 sc (30 sc total)

RND 7: 2 sc, 1 inc [4 sc, 1 inc] 5 times, 2 sc (36 sc total)

RND 8–17: 36 sc (10 rounds, [36 sc in each round])

RND 18: 2 sc, 1 dec [4 sc, 1 dec] 5 times, 2 sc (30 sc total)

RND 19: 30 sc (30 sc total)

Cut yarn but leave a long tail for sewing.

Embroider a black mouth in the middle of round 13 using black embroidery floss.

Attach a pair of 5-mm safety eyes between rounds 11 and 13 with 5 st between them.

Embroider black eyebrows using black embroidery floss and pink cheeks using Pink yarn.

Stuff your Daddy Succulent, and pin it to the side of the Pot. Sew it on.

MOMMY SUCCULENT

Using your Green yarn, start with a magic ring.

RND 1: 6 sc into the magic ring (6 sc total)

RND 2: [1 inc] 6 times (12 sc total)

RND 3: [1 sc, 1 inc] 6 times (18 sc total)

RND 4: 1 sc, 1 inc [2 sc, 1 inc] 5 times, 1 sc (24 sc total)

RND 5: 24 sc (24 sc total)

RND 6: [3 sc, 1 inc] 6 times (30 sc total)

RND 7–15: 30 sc (9 rounds, [30 sc in each round])

RND 16: [3 sc, 1 dec] 6 times (24 sc total)

RND 17: 24 sc (24 sc total)

Cut yarn but leave a long tail for sewing.

Embroider a black mouth in the middle of round 11 using black embroidery floss.

Attach a pair of 5-mm safety eyes between rounds 9 and 10 with 4 st between them.

Embroider black eyelashes using black embroidery floss and pink cheeks using Pink yarn.

Stuff your Mommy Succulent, and pin it next to your Daddy Succulent. Sew it on.

BABY SUCCULENT

Using your Green yarn, start with a magic ring.

RND 1: 6 sc into the magic ring (6 sc total)

RND 2: [1 inc] 6 times (12 sc total)

RND 3: [1 sc, 1 inc] 6 times (18 sc total)

RND 4: 1 sc, 1 inc [2 sc, 1 inc] 5 times, 1 sc (24 sc total)

RND 5–10: 24 sc (6 rounds, [24 sc in each round])

RND 11: 1 sc, 1 dec [2 sc, 1 dec] 5 times, 1 sc (18 sc total)

Cut yarn but leave a long tail for sewing.

Embroider a black mouth in the middle of round 6 using black embroidery floss.

Attach a pair of 4-mm safety eyes between rounds 5 and 6 with 4 st between them.

Embroider pink cheeks using Pink yarn.

Stuff your Baby Succulent, and pin it in front of your Mommy and Daddy Succulents. Sew it on.

BOW

Using your Pink yarn, start with a magic ring but don't pull it together.

Ch 3, 3 dc, ch 3, 1 sl, ch 3, 3 dc, ch 3, 1 sl into the ring.

Pull the magic ring closed.

Cut the yarn but leave an 8-inch (20-cm)-long yarn tail. Pull the yarn tail around the middle of the Bow a couple of times until you think it looks good.

Sew the Bow onto the side of your Mommy Succulent.

Cute & Cuddly Cactus

This Cute & Cuddly Cactus is quite an easy make, and you will be able to cuddle with it after you're done! You will first make the pot and soil together, then you'll crochet the three cactus pieces and sew them on. You know what would look so nice? A whole windowsill of Cute & Cuddly Cacti in pots featuring all the colors of the rainbow! That's on my to-do list for sure—how about yours?

SKILL LEVEL: BEGINNER

MATERIALS
Light fingering weight yarn in Pink, Brown, Hot Pink and Green
US B/1 (2.25-mm) hook
Tapestry needle
Black embroidery floss
A pair of 7-mm safety eyes
A small piece of cardboard
Polyester stuffing

ABBREVIATIONS
rnd: round
ch: chain
sc: single crochet
1 inc: single crochet 2 stitches into the same stitch
1 dec: single crochet 2 stitches together
sl: slip stitch
st(s): stitch(es)

Approximate size for a finished Cute & Cuddly Cactus: 4.3 x 3 inches (11 x 8 cm)

Cute & Cuddly Cactus Pattern

POT
Using your Pink yarn, start with a magic ring.

RND 1: 6 sc into the magic ring (6 sc total)

RND 2: [1 inc] 6 times (12 sc total)

RND 3: [1 sc, 1 inc] 6 times (18 sc total)

RND 4: 1 sc, 1 inc [2 sc, 1 inc] 5 times, 1 sc (24 sc total)

RND 5: [3 sc, 1 inc] 6 times (30 sc total)

RND 6: 2 sc, 1 inc [4 sc, 1 inc] 5 times, 2 sc (36 sc total)

RND 7: [5 sc, 1 inc] 6 times (42 sc total)

RND 8: In back loops only, 42 sc (42 sc total)

RND 9: 42 sc (42 sc total)

RND 10: 3 sc, 1 inc [6 sc, 1 inc] 5 times, 3 sc (48 sc total)

RND 11–12: 48 sc (2 rounds, [48 sc in each round])

RND 13: [7 sc, 1 inc] 6 times (54 sc total)

Rejoin your Brown yarn in one of the back loops of Rnd 21 on the Pot.

Work Rnd 1 for the soil in the remaining back loops of Rnd 21.

Here is what your piece should look like after you have worked the full soil round.

RND 14–19: 54 sc (6 rounds, [54 sc in each round])

RND 20: [7 sc, 1 dec] 6 times (48 sc total)

RND 21: In front loops only, 48 sc (48 sc total)

RND 22: 48 sc (48 sc total)

Finish with 1 sl.

Cut yarn and fasten off all threads.

Embroider a mouth in the middle of round 15 using black embroidery floss.

Attach a pair of 7-mm safety eyes between rounds 16 and 17 with 6 st apart.

Put your work on a piece of cardboard and cut out a piece that's the same size as the bottom. Place the cardboard piece in the bottom of the Pot. This will give more stability to your cactus Pot.

SOIL

Using your Brown yarn, rejoin in one of the back loops of round 21 on the Pot.

RND 1: In remaining back loops of round 21, 3 sc, 1 dec [6 sc, 1 dec] 5 times, 3 sc (42 sc total)

RND 2: [5 sc, 1 dec] 6 times (36 sc total)

RND 3: 2 sc, 1 dec [4 sc, 1 dec] 5 times, 2 sc (30 sc total)

Start stuffing, referring to the guide on page 11.

RND 4: [3 sc, 1 dec] 6 times (24 sc total)

RND 5: 1 sc, 1 dec [2 sc, 1 dec] 5 times, 1 sc (18 sc total)

RND 6: [1 sc, 1 dec] 6 times (12 sc total)

RND 7: [1 dec] 6 times (6 sc total)

Cut yarn and fasten off all threads.

CHEEKS (MAKE 2)

Using your Hot Pink yarn, start with a magic ring.

RND 1: 6 sc into the magic ring (6 sc total)

Finish with 1 sl.

Cut yarn but leave a long tail for sewing. Pin the Cheeks to the Pot and sew them on.

MAIN CACTUS

Using your Green yarn, ch 13.

ROW 1: Starting in the second ch from the hook, 12 sc, ch 1 (does not count as st throughout), and turn (12 sc total).

ROW 2–15: In back loops only, 12 sc, ch 1 and turn (14 rows, [12 sc in each row])

Cut yarn but leave a long tail for sewing.

Sew the two long sides together, then sew the top of the Cactus together. You may need to do a couple of stitches on the top to close it.

Stuff the Cactus and pin it in the middle of the Pot. Sew it on.

SIDE CACTI (MAKE 2)

Using your Green yarn, ch 10.

ROW 1: Starting in the second ch from the hook, 9 sc, ch 1 (does not count as st throughout), and turn (9 sc total).

ROW 2–9: In back loops only, 9 sc, ch 1 and turn (11 rows, [9 sc in each row])

Cut yarn but leave a long tail for sewing.

Sew the two long sides together, then sew the top of the Cactus together. You may need to do a couple of stitches on the top to close it.

Stuff the Side Cacti pieces and pin them on each side of the Main Cactus. Sew them on.

Cheeky Unicorn Cactus

If you ask me, you can turn pretty much anything into a unicorn, so why not make a Cheeky Unicorn Cactus? This doll is made in separate pieces, with the roses being my personal favorite. If you want to make this project a little more magical, why not use some glitter yarn for the pot?

SKILL LEVEL: INTERMEDIATE

MATERIALS

Light fingering weight yarn in Yellow, Brown, Green, Hot Pink, Gray, Light Blue, Pink and Lilac

US B/1 (2.25-mm) hook

A small piece of cardboard

Tapestry needle

Black embroidery floss

One 6-mm safety eye

Polyester stuffing

ABBREVIATIONS

rnd: round

ch: chain

sc: single crochet

1 inc: single crochet 2 stitches into the same stitch

1 dec: single crochet 2 stitches together

sl: slip stitch

st(s): stitch(es)

Approximate size for a finished Cheeky Unicorn Cactus: 5 x 4.7 inches (13 x 12 cm)

Cheeky Unicorn Cactus Pattern

POT

Using your Yellow yarn, start with a magic ring.

RND 1: 6 sc into the magic ring (6 sc total)

RND 2: [1 inc] 6 times (12 sc total)

RND 3: [1 sc, 1 inc] 6 times (18 sc total)

RND 4: 1 sc, 1 inc [2 sc, 1 inc] 5 times, 1 sc (24 sc total)

RND 5: [3 sc, 1 inc] 6 times (30 sc total)

RND 6: 2 sc, 1 inc [4 sc, 1 inc] 5 times, 2 sc (36 sc total)

RND 7: In back loops only, 36 sc (36 sc total)

RND 8–9: 36 sc (2 rounds, [36 sc in each round])

RND 10: [5 sc, 1 inc] 6 times (42 sc total)

RND 11–13: 42 sc (3 rounds, [42 sc in each round])

RND 14: 3 sc, 1 inc [6 sc, 1 inc] 5 times, 3 sc (48 sc total)

RND 15–17: 48 sc (3 rounds, [48 sc in each round])

RND 18: In front loops only, 48 sc (48 sc total)

RND 19: 48 sc (48 sc total)

Finish with 1 sl.

Cut yarn and fasten off all threads.

Put your work on a piece of cardboard and cut out a piece that's the same size as the bottom. Place the cardboard piece in the bottom of the Pot, to give it more stability.

SOIL

Using your Brown yarn, rejoin in one of the back loops of round 18 on the Pot.

RND 1: In remaining back loops of round 18, 3 sc, 1 dec [6 sc, 1 dec] 5 times, 3 sc (42 sc total)

RND 2: [5 sc, 1 dec] 6 times (36 sc total)

RND 3: 2 sc, 1 dec [4 sc, 1 dec] 5 times, 2 sc (30 sc total)

Start stuffing, referring to the guide on page 11.

RND 4: [3 sc, 1 dec] 6 times (24 sc total)

RND 5: 1 sc, 1 dec [2 sc, 1 dec] 5 times, 1 sc (18 sc total)

RND 6: [1 sc, 1 dec] 6 times (12 sc total)

RND 7: [1 dec] 6 times (6 sc total)

Cut yarn and fasten off all threads.

UNICORN CACTUS

Using your Green yarn, start with a magic ring.

RND 1: 6 sc into the magic ring (6 sc total)

RND 2: [1 inc] 6 times (12 sc total)

RND 3: [1 sc, 1 inc] 6 times (18 sc total)

RND 4: 1 sc, 1 inc [2 sc, 1 inc] 5 times, 1 sc (24 sc total)

RND 5: [3 sc, 1 inc] 6 times (30 sc total)

RND 6: 2 sc, 1 inc [4 sc, 1 inc] 5 times, 2 sc (36 sc total)

RND 7–19: 36 sc (13 rounds, [36 sc in each round])

RND 20: 2 sc, 1 dec [4 sc, 1 dec] 5 times, 2 sc (30 sc total)

Finish with 1 sl.

Cut yarn but leave a long tail for sewing.

Embroider a mouth in the middle of round 14 using black embroidery floss.

Attach one 6-mm safety eye between rounds 12 and 13; embroider a winking eye using your black embroidery floss about 5 st away from the safety eye.

Stuff the Cheeky Unicorn Cactus and pin it in the middle of the Pot. Sew it on.

ARMS (MAKE 2)

Using your Green yarn, start with a magic ring.

RND 1: 6 sc into the magic ring (6 sc total)

RND 2: [1 inc] 6 times (12 sc total)

RND 3–4: 12 sc (2 rounds, [12 sc in each round])

RND 5: [1 dec] 2 times, 3 sc, [1 inc] 2 times, 3 sc (12 sc total)

RND 6: [1 dec] 2 times, 3 sc, [1 inc] 2 times, 3 sc (12 sc total)

RND 7–10: 12 sc (4 rounds, [12 sc in each round])

Finish with 1 sl.

Cut yarn but leave a long tail for sewing.

Stuff the Arms and pin them to the Cheeky Unicorn Cactus. Sew them on.

EARS (MAKE 2)

Using your Green yarn, start with a magic ring.

RND 1: 6 sc into the magic ring (6 sc total)

RND 2: 6 sc (6 sc total)

RND 3: [1 inc] 6 times (12 sc total)

RND 4–5: 12 sc (2 rounds, [12 sc in each round])

RND 6: [1 sc, 1 dec] 4 times (8 sc total)

Finish with 1 sl.

Cut yarn but leave a long tail for sewing.

Pin the Ears to the Cheeky Unicorn Cactus and sew them on.

CHEEKS (MAKE 2)

Using your Hot Pink yarn, start with a magic ring.

RND 1: 6 sc into the magic ring (6 sc total)

Finish with 1 sl.

Cut yarn but leave a long tail for sewing. Pin the Cheeks to the Cheeky Unicorn Cactus and sew them on.

UNICORN HORN

Using your Gray yarn, start with a magic ring.

RND 1: 6 sc into the magic ring (6 sc total)

RND 2: 6 sc (6 sc total)

RND 3: [1 sc, 1 inc] 3 times (9 sc total)

RND 4–6: 9 sc (3 rounds [9 sc in each round])

Finish with 1 sl.

Cut yarn but leave a long tail for sewing.

Pin the Horn to the Cheeky Unicorn Cactus and sew it on.

ROSES (MAKE 3)

Using your Light Blue yarn, ch 8.

ROW 1: Starting in the second ch from the hook, 2 sc in each st, ch 1 (does not count as st), and turn. (14 sc total)

ROW 2: 2 sc in each st (28 sc total)

Roll the piece into a rose shape and sew the piece together so it doesn't unroll.

Repeat with your Pink and Lilac yarns for a total of three Roses. Pin the Roses to the Cheeky Unicorn Cactus and sew them on.

Charming Bunny Cactus

For a special springtime piece, you can make a cactus into a bunny! The pot is made first, then you make the Charming Bunny Cactus. The main piece of the cactus is crocheted in rows and not in rounds so that you'll have a long piece that you then sew together. This construction is a little bit different from the other pieces in this chapter, but that doesn't make it any less fun.

SKILL LEVEL: INTERMEDIATE

MATERIALS

Light fingering weight yarn in Light Blue, Light Pink, Brown, Green, Pink and Hot Pink
US B/1 (2.25-mm) hook
A small piece of cardboard
Tapestry needle
Black embroidery floss
A pair of 6-mm safety eyes
Polyester stuffing

ABBREVIATIONS

rnd: round
ch: chain
sc: single crochet
1 inc: single crochet 2 stitches into the same stitch
1 dec: single crochet 2 stitches together
sl: slip stitch
st(s): stitch(es)

Approximate size for a finished Charming Bunny Cactus: 6.6 x 2.7 inches (17 x 7 cm)

Charming Bunny Cactus Pattern

POT

Using your Light Blue yarn, start with a magic ring.

RND 1: 6 sc into the magic ring (6 sc total)

RND 2: [1 inc] 6 times (12 sc total)

RND 3: [1 sc, 1 inc] 6 times (18 sc total)

RND 4: 1 sc, 1 inc [2 sc, 1 inc] 5 times, 1 sc (24 sc total)

RND 5: [3 sc, 1 inc] 6 times (30 sc total)

RND 6: 2 sc, 1 inc [4 sc, 1 inc] 5 times, 2 sc (36 sc total)

RND 7: In back loops only, 36 sc (36 sc total)

RND 8–9: 36 sc (2 rounds, [36 sc in each round])

RND 10: [5 sc, 1 inc] 6 times (42 sc total)

Change to Light Pink.

RND 11: 42 sc (42 sc total)

Change to Light Blue.

RND 12–13: 42 sc (2 rounds, [42 sc in each round])

RND 14: 3 sc, 1 inc [6 sc, 1 inc] 5 times, 3 sc (48 sc total)

Change to Light Pink.

RND 15: 48 sc (48 sc total)

Change to Light Blue.

RND 16–18: 48 sc (3 rounds, [48 sc in each round])

RND 19: In front loops only, 48 sc (48 sc total)

Change to Light Pink.

RND 20: *4 sc in the next st, skip 1 st, 1 sl, skip 1 st*

Repeat from * to * for the entire round.

Finish with 1 sl.

Cut yarn and fasten off all threads.

Put your work on a piece of cardboard and cut out a piece that's the same size as the bottom. Place the cardboard piece in the bottom of the Pot. This will give more stability to your cactus Pot.

SOIL

Using your Brown yarn, rejoin in one of the back loops of round 19 on the Pot.

RND 1: In remaining back loops of round 19, 3 sc, 1 dec [6 sc, 1 dec] 5 times, 3 sc (42 sc total)

RND 2: [5 sc, 1 dec] 6 times (36 sc total)

RND 3: 2 sc, 1 dec [4 sc, 1 dec] 5 times, 2 sc (30 sc total)

Start stuffing, referring to the guide on page 11.

RND 4: [3 sc, 1 dec] 6 times (24 sc total)

RND 5: 1 sc, 1 dec [2 sc, 1 dec] 5 times, 1 sc (18 sc total)

RND 6: [1 sc, 1 dec] 6 times (12 sc total)

RND 7: [1 dec] 6 times (6 sc total)

Cut yarn and fasten off all threads.

BUNNY CACTUS

Using your Green yarn, ch 25.

ROW 1: Starting in the second ch from the hook, 24 sc, ch 1 (does not count as st), and turn (24 sc total).

ROW 2–33: In back loops only, 24 sc and turn (32 rows, [24 sc in each row])

Cut yarn but leave a long tail for sewing.

Sew the two long sides together, then sew the top of the Bunny Cactus together. You may need to do a couple of stitches on the top to close it.

Embroider a mouth using black embroidery floss.

Attach a pair of 6-mm safety eyes 5 rows apart.

Stuff the Cactus and pin it in the middle of the Pot. Sew it on.

BUNNY EARS (MAKE 2)

Using your Green yarn, start with a magic ring.

RND 1: 6 sc into the magic ring (6 sc total)

RND 2: 6 sc (6 sc total)

RND 3: [1 inc] 6 times (12 sc total)

RND 4–10: 12 sc (7 rounds, [12 sc in each round])

RND 11: [1 dec] 6 times (6 sc total)

Finish with 1 sl.

Cut yarn but leave a long tail for sewing.

Pin the Ears to the Bunny Cactus and sew them on.

After Rnd 23, your Bunny Cactus piece should look like this. Sew the two long sides together.

Sew the top of the Bunny Cactus together.

After you have sewn it together, your piece should look like this.

CHEEKS (MAKE 2)

Using your Pink yarn, start with a magic ring.

RND 1: 6 sc into the magic ring (6 sc total)

Finish with 1 sl.

Cut yarn but leave a long tail for sewing. Pin the Cheeks to the Bunny Cactus and sew them on.

FLOWER

Using your Hot Pink yarn, start with a magic ring.

RND 1: 5 sc into the magic ring (5 sc total)

RND 2: [1 sl, 1 sc, 1 dc, 1 sc, 1 sl] in each st around

Finish with 1 sl.

Cut yarn but leave a long tail for sewing. Pin the Flower on top of the Bunny Cactus and sew it on.

Aloe-You-Vera Much

This cute aloe vera plant will make your heart melt! It does take some time to make, but it is all worth it in the end! You will first crochet the pot, then you'll make the leaves separately before sewing everything together. Beat the heat and show a special someone how much you care with this soothing project.

SKILL LEVEL: BEGINNER

MATERIALS

Light fingering weight yarn in Lilac, Light Green, Brown and Hot Pink

US B/1 (2.25-mm) hook

Tapestry needle

Black embroidery floss

A pair of 6-mm safety eyes

A small piece of cardboard

Polyester stuffing

ABBREVIATIONS

rnd: round

ch: chain

sc: single crochet

1 inc: single crochet 2 stitches into the same stitch

1 dec: single crochet 2 stitches together

dc: double crochet

sl: slip stitch

st(s): stitch(es)

Approximate size for a finished Aloe-You-Vera Much: 4.7 x 3 inches (12 x 8 cm)

Aloe-You-Vera Much Pattern

POT

Using your Lilac yarn, start with a magic ring.

RND 1: 6 sc into the magic ring (6 sc total)

RND 2: [1 inc] 6 times (12 sc total)

RND 3: [1 sc, 1 inc] 6 times (18 sc total)

RND 4: 1 sc, 1 inc [2 sc, 1 inc] 5 times, 1 sc (24 sc total)

RND 5: [3 sc, 1 inc] 6 times (30 sc total)

RND 6: 2 sc, 1 inc [4 sc, 1 inc] 5 times, 2 sc (36 sc total)

RND 7: [5 sc, 1 inc] 6 times (42 sc total)

RND 8: In back loops only, 42 sc (42 sc total)

RND 9-10: 42 sc (2 rounds [42 sc in each round])

RND 11: 3 sc, 1 inc [6 sc, 1 inc] 5 times, 3 sc (48 sc total)

RND 12-13: 48 sc (2 rounds [48 sc in each round])

RND 14: [7 sc, 1 inc] 6 times (54 sc total)

RND 15-19: 54 sc (5 rounds [54 sc in each round])

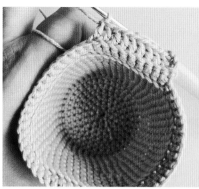
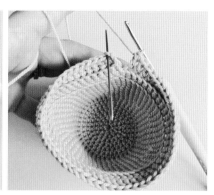

Turn the Pot around so that you have the opening against you.

Working in the back loops only, 1 dc in each st to the end of the row.

Finish with 1 sl.

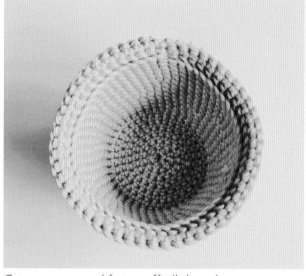

Fold Rnd 22 over the Pot toward the outside edge.

Cut your yarn and fasten off all threads.

RND 20: In front loops only, 54 sc (54 sc total)

RND 21: 54 sc (54 sc total)

Turn the Pot around so that you have the opening against you. Now you are going to crochet in the back loops.

RND 22: In back loops only, ch 3, 1 dc in each st to the end of the row (54 sc total)

Finish with 1 sl.

Fold round 22 over the Pot.

Cut yarn and fasten off all threads.

Embroider a mouth in the middle of round 14.

Attach a pair of 6-mm safety eyes between rounds 15 and 16 with 5 st between them.

Put your work on a piece of cardboard and cut out a piece that's the same size as the bottom. Place the cardboard piece in the bottom of the Pot. This will give more stability to your cactus Pot.

SOIL

Using your Brown yarn, rejoin in one of the back loops of round 20 on the Pot.

RND 1: In remaining back loops of round 20, [7 sc, 1 dec] 6 times (48 sc total)

RND 2: 3 sc, 1 dec [6 sc, 1 dec] 5 times, 3 sc (42 sc total)

RND 3: [5 sc, 1 dec] 6 times (36 sc total)

RND 4: 2 sc, 1 dec [4 sc, 1 dec] 5 times, 2 sc (30 sc total)

Start stuffing, referring to the guide on page 11.

RND 5: [3 sc, 1 dec] 6 times (24 sc total)

RND 6: 1 sc, 1 dec [2 sc, 1 dec] 5 times, 1 sc (18 sc total)

RND 7: [1 sc, 1 dec] 6 times (12 sc total)

RND 8: [1 dec] 6 times (6 sc total)

Cut yarn and fasten off all threads.

CHEEKS (MAKE 2)

Using your Hot Pink yarn, start with a magic ring.

RND 1: 6 sc into the magic ring (6 sc total)

Finish with 1 sl.

Cut yarn but leave a long tail for sewing. Pin the Cheeks to the Pot and sew them on.

LONG LEAVES (MAKE 2)

Using your Light Green yarn, start with a magic ring.

RND 1: 6 sc into the magic ring (6 sc total)

RND 2: 6 sc (6 sc total)

RND 3: [1 inc] 6 times (12 sc total)

RND 4–17: 12 sc (14 rounds, [12 sc in each round])

Finish with 1 sl.

Cut yarn but leave a long tail for sewing.

Press the Long Leaves flat with your hands, if necessary, and pin them in the middle of the Pot and sew them on.

MIDDLE LEAVES (MAKE 5)

Using your Light Green yarn, start with a magic ring.

RND 1: 6 sc into the magic ring (6 sc total)

RND 2: 6 sc (6 sc total)

RND 3: [1 inc] 6 times (12 sc total)

RND 4–15: 12 sc (12 rounds, [12 sc in each round])

Finish with 1 sl.

Cut yarn but leave a long tail for sewing.

Press the Middle Leaves flat with your hands, if necessary, and pin them on the outside of the Long Leaves and sew them on.

SHORT LEAVES (MAKE 8)

Using your Light Green yarn, start with a magic ring.

RND 1: 6 sc into the magic ring (6 sc total)

RND 2: 6 sc (6 sc total)

RND 3: [1 inc] 6 times (12 sc total)

RND 4–13: 12 sc (10 rounds, [12 sc in each round])

Finish with 1 sl.

Cut yarn but leave a long tail for sewing.

Press the Short Leaves flat with your hands, if necessary, and pin them on the outside of the Middle Leaves and sew them on.

ACKNOWLEDGMENTS

· ·

I'd like to thank everyone who made this book possible: my family, who always supports me in everything I do, and especially Emily Taylor at Page Street Publishing. She has been a huge help in the making of this book, and I have loved working with her. Thank you to the rest of the Page Street Publishing team for bringing my book to life! I'd also like to send a huge thanks to Cara Medus for all her work on the tech editing of these patterns. It has been a pleasure working with her. And to the many crafters who have supported my shop and made my patterns over the years, thank you so much!

ABOUT THE AUTHOR

· ·

Jennifer Santos is the amigurumi artist behind Super Cute Design and the founder of Super Cute Design Shop, an online store where she sells her amigurumi patterns. With an eye for the adorable and an audience of over 140,000 on Instagram, Jennifer is known in the crochet community for her bright, colorful, intricate amigurumi designs.

Jennifer's work and patterns have been featured by *Simply Crochet* magazine, *Inside Crochet* magazine and *Mollie Makes* magazine. She currently lives in Sweden with her husband, two kids and two cats.

You can find Jennifer on Instagram @supercutedesign, and you can find more of her patterns in her Etsy shop: www.SuperCuteDesignShop.etsy.com.

INDEX